WITH THE COMPLIMENTS OF
ANGLO AMERICAN FARMS LIMITED

BOSCHENDAL
WHERE THE FRENCH HUGUENOTS FIRST GREW WINE

VERGELEGEN
ANNO 1700

CAPE WINES

BODY & SOUL

FERNWOOD PRESS
P O Box 15344
8018 Vlaeberg

Registration no. 90/04463/07

First published 1997

Text © Graham Knox 1997
Photographs © Alain Proust 1997, with the exception of the following: Colin Paterson-Jones p.79/5; WINE magazine/Peter van Niekerk p.93/4.

Edited by Leni Martin
Designed and typeset by Alix Gracie
Dustjacket design by Willem Jordaan
Map by Silverhammer
Repro co-ordinator Andrew de Kock
Printed and bound by Tien Wah Press (Pte) Ltd, Singapore

ISBN 1 874950 31 8

Photography by Alain Proust · Text by Graham Knox

CAPE WINES

BODY & SOUL

CONTENTS

The pale green coloration on the map represents vineyard areas.

The elegant Cape Dutch homestead of Zevenwacht stands below the estate's newly planted vineyards.

ATLANTIC OCEAN

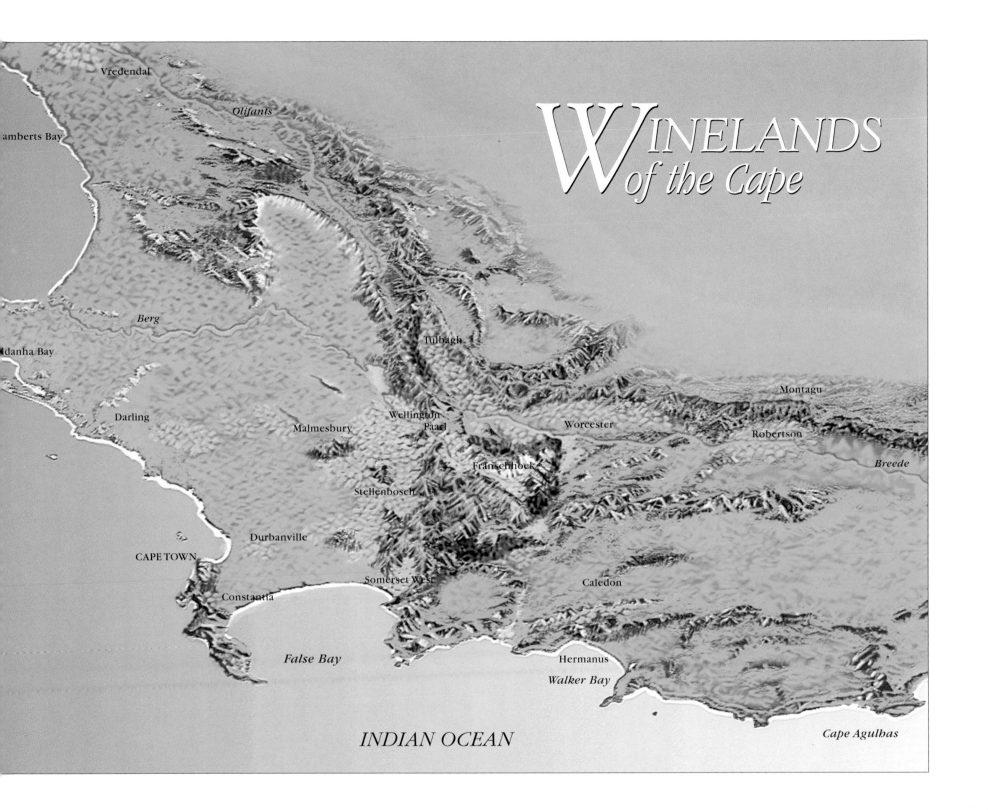

WINELANDS of the Cape

Vredendal
Olifants
amberts Bay
Berg
Tulbagh
danha Bay
Montagu
Darling
Wellington
Malmesbury
Paarl
Worcester
Robertson
Franschhoek
Breede
Stellenbosch
Durbanville
CAPE TOWN
Somerset West
Caledon
Constantia
False Bay
Hermanus
Walker Bay
INDIAN OCEAN
Cape Agulhas

ACKNOWLEDGEMENTS

Any subject as diverse as South African wine, viewed from all directions, needs input from people with many fields of expertise.
I have to thank everyone who encouraged and supported me, and who contributed or corrected the information you will find on these pages.
If I try to be comprehensive, I'll probably overlook someone, but I want to draw attention to the valuable assistance provided by a few marvellously
helpful people, who are listed in no particular order: Vanessa Pearce, Leni Martin, Sterik de Wet, Frans Malan, Germaine Grammer, Rob Lawrie,
Di Knox, Dawie le Roux, Buks Venter, Nienke Esterhuizen, Eve Jell, Derick Henstra, Tony Gouveia and, of course, Pieter Struik, who
said he wanted a book, and Alain Proust, who said he had lots of pictures. Thank you everyone who helped.

GRAHAM KNOX, CAPE TOWN, JULY 1997

The Cape – that borderless southwestern part of South Africa that was first settled by Europeans and later became a British colony – is blessed with spectacular countryside and a 300-year history of producing wine. Its position at the tip of a continent, a mild, mediterranean climate and mountainous terrain all contribute to the making of fine wines, a tradition that has seen peaks and troughs since the days of the great Constantia wine renowned throughout eighteenth-century Europe. An exploration of the region's mountains and valleys, its cellars and vineyards reveals the origins of its reputation for fine wine.

THE CAPE

Winelands

1

The provisions of nature

During summer the sun rises late and sets early behind the peaks in the prime wine-producing vineyards of South Africa's mountainous southwestern Cape. Whether you face east or west, a range will be looming behind or in front of you, casting its own shadow across its slopes. In midsummer there are some vineyards that see the sun rising above the peaked horizons only at ten in the morning. Once it has cleared the highest summits, though, the transition from shade to light is abrupt and, as if to make up for lost time, the intensity of the sunlight is overwhelmingly strong. Gabled white homesteads stand starkly outlined against the soft greens of surrounding oaks.

When one considers other areas of the world that produce fine wines, the Cape vineyards, at about 34°S, are comparatively close to the equator. On the Cape's longest day of the year, in December, they receive a maximum of 14 hours of sunlight. On the same date the sun shines on Melbourne in Australia (latitude 38°S) for 14.5 hours, and in Bordeaux (latitude 45°N) it shines for nearly 16 hours on 22 June.

The Cape winelands, located mainly in the Western Cape province of South Africa, are centred around the towns of Stellenbosch, Paarl and Franschhoek in the 'Boland', or 'upper land', but extend westwards through Durbanville and into the Constantia valley on the Cape Peninsula; northwards to the middle and lower reaches of the Olifants River; southwards to

3

4

(Previous page) Lanzerac, Stellenbosch. 1. Snow falls regularly each winter on mountain peaks in the Cape's wine country, but seldom in the vineyards.
2. Vines have been planted in soil where the Cape's indigenous flora, such as these proteas, grew for thousands of years.

3. The Constantia valley is situated on a narrow neck of land between the Atlantic and Indian oceans, its vines cooled by sea breezes. 4. Cape mountains cast heavy shadow over the vineyards in the mornings or late afternoon, restricting the number of hours that sunlight falls on the grapes.

1

Walker Bay and Hermanus; and eastwards along the Breede River and beyond, penetrating deep into the Little Karoo. An offshoot along the Orange River yields large quantities of grapes on deep, fertile and well-irrigated soils.

Positioned as they are at the southwestern tip of a vast continent that spans the equator and both the tropics, the winelands occupy a mediterranean climatic zone, where rain falls mostly in winter and dry summers with a low humidity level allow grapes to ripen evenly and reliably, developing to full-flavoured succulence. About the same size as Scotland, they enjoy a moderate climate that is, on occasion, subjected to bouts of fury. In winter fierce north-westerly gales may bring rainstorms that lash the countryside, but in general the winter weather is not unlike that of western Europe in spring or autumn – cool and damp, interspersed with bright and sunny days that often provide a generous degree of warmth. Snow regularly dusts the highest peaks, but night-time temperatures in winter seldom fall below freezing point and frost damage is rarely one of a Cape wine-farmer's concerns.

In relation to other parts of southern Africa, the southwestern Cape's rainfall is high, thanks to oceanic and topographical influences. The annual precipitation along the coastal plain, averaging 555 millimetres and occurring mainly between the months of May and September, is sufficient to allow plants to grow and maintain foliage year after year. Compared with other wine-growing regions around the world, though, the average winter rainfall in the most damp of all the Cape's vineyards is lower than that of any part of Burgundy, Champagne or Bordeaux. Almost all of them need at least a little supplementary water in summer to bring a healthy crop of grapes to fruition. For many vine-growers, particularly those in the semi-arid regions, a regular and permanent supply of irrigation water is an essential element of cultivation.

COMPETING WITH THE DEVIL

Popular lore maintains that the 'tablecloth' covering Table Mountain when the southeaster blows is not, as the meteorologists would have it, a layer of cloud. The explanation is far more intriguing.

Centuries ago retired pirate Van Hunks was sitting on Devil's Peak smoking his long clay pipe in contemplative mood. When a stranger approached and asked him for some tobacco, Van Hunks was happy to oblige. As the two sat puffing away contentedly, the stranger boasted that he could blow greater clouds of smoke than his companion could. The stranger – none other than the devil – was greatly put out when Van Hunks proved to have the more powerful lungs. Ever since that day the two have been locked in relentless contest, blowing vast swathes of smoke across the top of Table Mountain on a summer's day.

1. As a visual indicator of summer, the southeasterly wind creates a regular white tablecloth on the Franschhoek mountains.

2. Morning mists in summer provide precious moisture in west coast vineyards.

2

3

The intensity of the summer sunlight and the southwestern Cape's relative proximity to the equator should, in theory, combine to create extreme temperatures which would be fatal to the production of good wine. Although in summer peak temperatures in the main vine-growing areas are high and grapes ripen easily, days of excessive heat are rare. Two factors are responsible for tempering the heat: the proximity of most Western Cape wine-growing areas to a coast, and the 'Cape Doctor', the southeasterly wind which blows, often with extravagant fury, across the southwestern Cape throughout spring and summer.

Most of the Cape's weather, including its fabled southeasterly wind, originates from barometric pressure zones and perennial wind patterns that are continually advancing on the southern end of the continent. In summer a high-pressure zone regularly develops over the continental shelf at the southern tip of Africa, an area of warm water and unpredictable currents known as the Agulhas Bank. From this region a stream of wind, sometimes mild, occasionally tempestuous, flows in a northwesterly direction across the rows of vines with their burden of grapes towards the low-pressure zone over the Atlantic. This wind, together with a variation that blows in from the southwest, dominates both the macro-climate (the weather) and the micro-climate (the environment around each vine) of the whole wine-growing region during summer, its ventilating effect inhibiting the development of vineyard diseases.

The southeaster only occasionally brings rain to the coastal vineyards and even more rarely dumps moisture on the vineyards beyond the first range of mountains. However, it has a moderating influence on the temperature of what, in its absence, would have been the hottest days of summer, lowering the potential maximum by several degrees. It also has an extraordinary visual perspective, being visible in the form of a seemingly tangible white cloud

4

3. Southeast cloud condensing on the mountains makes an important contribution to the Cape's climate.
4. Fog drifts into ripening vineyards from the west coast's cold Benguela current.

13

as it crests over a northwest-facing mountain. The humidity in the advancing wind, though comparatively low, condenses as it meets the thermal updraft on the mountain's face and creates a continuously flowing, luminous white cascade that falls for hours, sometimes even days, on end.

Cooling breezes are not the only benefit that proximity to the coast brings to Cape vineyards. The seas off the southwestern corner of Africa are the turbulent meeting-place of two opposing ocean currents: the Indian Ocean's Agulhas current which sweeps down the southeastern coast of southern Africa, and the Atlantic's Benguela current which dominates the climate and living conditions of the subcontinent's west coast.

The Agulhas current, flowing southwards from the tropics at the remarkable speed of five knots, or 2.6 metres per second, brings a warm-water flow into contact with the relatively dense, slow-moving, northerly drift of the icy Benguela current. Repelled by the denser, colder Benguela water and losing its immense energy and direction, the Agulhas stream turns eastward, flowing towards Australia as a segment of a perpetual counter-clockwise cycle. As it passes Cape Agulhas its temperature is around 23 °C in midsummer. Evaporation from this warm-water mass occurs at the point where the southeasterly winds developing around the southern rim of the South Atlantic high-pressure zone pick up speed as they race towards the Western Cape's agricultural areas, carrying with them a degree of humidity to the Cape's dry summer climate.

The water off the Western Cape's west coast is 10 °C colder in midsummer, and the temperature gradient between maximum and minimum, summer or winter, remains constant at

1

2

3

1. Breezes from the Indian Ocean, just five kilometres away, temper the heat in this hillside Sauvignon Blanc vineyard near Somerset West.

2. Traditionally the site of apple and pear orchards, the high-lying Elgin valley now also supports vineyards.

3. Snow dusts the mountain tops during the winter months in the Elgin valley. At this time of year
the vines are dormant, awaiting the warmer temperatures of spring.

1. The majority of the Cape's grapes, such as these in the Breede River valley, are grown in arid areas under irrigation.
2. Traditionally, irrigated inland vineyards were planted on the level floor of the river valley.

2

3

only 2 °C. In summer when the southeaster dies down, generally at night, an easterly onshore drift of air from over the Benguela current pushes onto the land a dense fog which blankets vineyards planted within a few kilometres of the chill west coast, soaking the ripening grapes as the sugar is rising in them and keeping temperatures low until nine or ten o'clock in the morning. Wine farms within reach of this ground-hugging mist have the opportunity to benefit from lower yields of grapes and intensified flavour, and among the wines produced at such farms was the 'Constantia' beloved by Napoleon Bonaparte and Jane Austen, and many of their contemporaries.

The Cape's mountains, as well as providing a dramatic backdrop to the landscape, play a more practical role by ensuring that the vineyards receive a good – though not always sufficient – supply of rain. Winter approaches the southwestern Cape from the west, from over the Atlantic. The prevailing moisture-bearing wind swings in from the northwest, in the opposite direction to the major wind of summer, and collides with the ridges and ranges of the mountain chains that form barriers roughly parallel to the southwestern and southern coasts. As the storm clouds are blown across the peaks they release their watery burden onto the slopes and valleys below and then roll on eastward, darkening the sky but carrying little moisture with them.

Although the valleys beyond the mountain ranges have fertile soils, the rain that falls on them is too poor and spasmodic to regularly sustain crops of grapes and must be supplemented. The agricultural bounty of Worcester, Robertson, Bonnievale and the Little Karoo depends on water being diverted from higher-rainfall areas and stored, to be made available on a daily basis, as the vineyards need it.

Vineyards along the Cape's west coast also need extensive irrigation. They receive little natural rainfall, as the prevailing winds all year are offshore and dry. These powerful winds

4

---

3. On the farm Mont Blois, in the Robertson valley, vines thrive on limestone-rich soils. 4. Mountain slopes and valleys far from the coast – such as the fertile Koo valley – are today being planted with vines.

1

move the surface coastal water northward and westward, causing an upwelling of permanently cold water from the ocean floor. The only westerly movement of air reaching most of the coast is the gentle onshore drift of fog which blankets the coastal lands when the dominant offshore winds die down. The thickest fogs and most intense desert conditions occur well north of Cape Town, where the offshore winds and the upwelling effect are strongest.

Sunshine, rainfall and cooling breezes all conspire to nurture the vines and their fruit, but a fourth − and perhaps most important − factor is the soil in which they grow. A healthy vine derives its nutrition from the soil and energy from sunlight, converting them into sugar and flavour components in the grape. This is a stressful task, achieved most successfully by a plant which is in peak health and rooted deep in moist, friable soil. In the question of a soil's fertility, too little is preferable to too much, for if a soil is too fertile the plant converts the nutrition derived from it into vegetative growth, enhancing its structure to the detriment of its fruit. Moderately fertile soils are best for vineyards, being rich enough to support a vine that, although retarded in its growth, has stamina to convert nature's earth-derived goodness into character and flavour in the grape.

3

2

1. Date palms indicate the desert-like climate of the Orange River vineyards, 800 kilometres north of Cape Town. 2. Rainfall decreases as one travels northward up the west coast. The vineyards at Darling are the most northerly ones near the coast which are not irrigated.

4

5

The Cape's soils derive chiefly from the three main rock types in the region, namely sandstone, granite and shale. Vines grow strongly in any of them, and when the soil has a moderate proportion of water-retaining clay to provide moisture in the dry summer months, they remain healthy all year round. Most of the Cape's agricultural land has a layer of topsoil which contains a proportion of clay, and this in turn rests on a bed of clay. In certain areas the topsoil contains an additional proportion of limestone-derived soil which generally has better acid-alkaline balance than clay soils. This balance is carried through into the grape juice and wines. Limestone also acts as sponge, soaking up water when it rains and releasing it during the dry times.

With so many positive natural factors contributing to South Africa's success as a wine-producing country, it is difficult to establish, some three and a half centuries after the event, whether the pioneers of today's wine industry recognised the land's potential from the beginning or whether they became aware of it as a matter of chance. It would certainly seem, though, that the man who first took wine-making in the Cape seriously, the commander and later governor of the Dutch colony, Simon van der Stel, knew what he was doing when he planted his vineyards at Constantia towards the end of the seventeenth century. The fact that the Cape has a wine-making tradition today can be attributed largely to him, controversial though he may have been.

3. Near Vredendal, lush vineyards grow in alluvial soil on the valley floor, and on the limestone hills to the left. 4. Water channelled from the Orange River is used to irrigate adjacent vineyards. 5. A canal carries water from the Olifants River Dam near Clanwilliam to irrigate vineyards near the river's mouth.

1

2

The first great vineyard outside Europe

The Constantia valley today, with its large, tree-shaded properties, is one of the most affluent of Cape Town's suburbs with land at a premium, yet it clings still to its vinicultural past and even, in places, is rejuvenating it. The cradle of the South African wine industry, the valley was the 'grand cru' territory of the Dutch and then English colony throughout the eighteenth and nineteenth centuries, obtaining for its wines much higher prices than did the next most valuable vineyard area. It also suffered less in periods of downturn. So special were the wines it produced that its economic fortunes were independent of those of other wine-producing parts of the colony; while the Cape's economy went through periods of boom and bust, Constantia wines were always in demand.

Wine-making at the Cape began with Jan van Riebeeck, the first commander of the victualling station set up by the Dutch East India Company (*Vereenigde Oost-Indische Compagnie*,

3

1. The eighteenth-century cellar at Groot Constantia is now a museum. Wine is made in an adjacent modern cellar. 2. The original Constantia vineyards were planted near both mountains and sea. In autumn, rain is seldom far away. 3. A detail from the original cellar's pediment, sculpted by immigrant German Anton Anreith.

5

or VOC) on the shores of Table Bay in 1652. He planted the first vines, and in 1659 made the first wine. In 1676 the colony's first trained wine-maker, Hannes Coekenberg, arrived and brought with him the first wine press.

When Simon van der Stel, the first of the young colony's administrators of note, arrived in 1679 he was critical of the farming settlers' clumsy methods of wine-making. His attitude coloured by his own interest in wine, he issued a quality-enforcing proclamation in which he assured the farmers that they would find their product '...notably improved if grapes were allowed to ripen [fully]'. Cellars would be '...visited by a committee and [sales would be permitted only if grapes were] pronounced by the committee to be of the requisite maturity'. Farmers who ignored his proclamation had financial penalties imposed on them.

Possibly to set an example for the Cape farmers, probably with an eye for his own gain, in 1685 Van der Stel persuaded his Dutch East India Company employers to override the law forbidding Company personnel from owning property or trading for personal benefit so that he could grant himself about 900 morgen (almost 800 hectares) of forested land in the Constantia valley, beyond Wynberg. It is tempting to conclude that when he chose Constantia, he recognised the quality inherent in the deep red soils, the gentle slopes and the oceanic influence on the valley's climate. Whether fortuitous or deliberate, Van der Stel's choice could not have been better. With the Company's slaves at his disposal, he cleared land, planted vines, and turned his property into a model vineyard. He pioneered the use of supports for his vines and the harvesting of fully ripe grapes, and employed a wine-maker he had brought out from Europe. So successful was he at wine-farming that as early as 1692 Constantia wine was referred to as 'special' and the 'best wine in the Cape'. In 1705 it sold for £20 per 160-gallon barrel, far above the price of other Cape wines. Constantia had become one of the great wine estates of the world, and the only one outside Europe.

The zenith of Constantia's fortunes was achieved under the stewardship of Hendrik Cloete, who bought the Cape Colony's most valuable farm in 1778. He established strict vineyard, harvesting and wine-making programmes that created one of the world's sweet wine classics that became known simply as 'Constantia'. Made from late-harvested, very ripe fruit fermented to around 13 per cent of alcohol, this richly flavoured, naturally fermented wine retained a high proportion of original grape sugar.

Renowned as 'Constantia' was, only a third of it was available to the commercial trade. First the Dutch East India Company administration and then its British successors ruled that the estate had to supply one third of each crop for the use of the Cape government and had to ship another third to administrative headquarters, originally in Holland and Batavia and subsequently in Britain. The wines that did reach Europe via the commercial trade could be found in the courts of Russia, Sweden, Britain, France and Prussia. They even occasionally graced the tables of privileged consumers in India, Ceylon, Australia and North America. When Napoleon was exiled to St Helena in 1816 he insisted on being supplied with Constantia, and each year until his death in 1821 he and his entourage drank the major portion of both the government's allocation and Cloete's own sales.

After more than a century in Cloete hands, Groot Constantia was sold in 1885 to the Colonial government for use as an experimental wine estate under the supervision of Baron Carl von Babo, an Austrian expert on viticulture. The farm's great wine-producing days had come to an end. Its fortunes faltered along with those of South Africa's wine industry as a whole, which was almost overwhelmed first by phylloxera in 1886, and then by the effects of the Anglo-Boer War. Today, wine-making at Constantia is undergoing a major renaissance, through the efforts of the current owners of parts of Van der Stel's original property.

6

4. Buitenverwachting is a subdivision of Van der Stel's original property. From the location of his farm (foreground) the Constantia vineyards have advanced up the mountain slope. 5. Twice rebuilt after fires, Groot Constantia's manor house is one of South Africa's chief tourist attractions. 6. A bottle of 'Constantia'.

2

3

4

1   5

6

Expansion into the Stellenbosch and Paarl districts

While Constantia's fortunes flourished in the seventeenth and eighteenth centuries, farmers elsewhere in the colony struggled to earn much of an income from making wine. The Cape's first European-style farms had been granted along the Liesbeek River in today's suburban Cape Town, but by the time Van der Stel arrived all these enterprises had failed. He sought an alternative location for agricultural development and found it in Stellenbosch's broad valley with its perennial water, and in the adjacent Paarl valley along the Berg River.

The first Stellenbosch farms were granted to the most diligent of the Dutch East India Company's indentured employees at the end of their contracts. Within two or three years of the granting of the Stellenbosch sites, all the prime land along Paarl's Berg River, in the area known today as Simondium and Groot Drakenstein, had been granted to other Dutch and German settlers. And between them, interspersed to prevent the development of an alien colony, individual farms were granted to the few dozen Huguenot families which had arrived at the Cape in 1688 and shortly afterwards.

Many of the new farmers were inexperienced, and they began their careers with little more than an axe, a few spades and several bags of seed as start-up capital. In accordance with Company policy, they were encouraged to grow grain, trade in livestock with the indigenous

---

1. The interior of Schreuder House, dating from 1709 and forming part of the Village Museum, gives a glimpse into early Stellenbosch life.
2. Artefacts from the old Cape are sold at Oom Samie se Winkel. 3. An elegant townhouse in Stellenbosch. 4. Junior league football on a Stellenbosch wine farm.
5. The Stellenryck Wine Museum. 6. Some of the Cape Dutch houses in Stellenbosch were embellished with Victorian-style verandahs a century ago.

1

2

people and supply food to the settlement on the shores of Table Bay. Visiting ships' crews brought a demand for alcohol that encouraged the farmers in Stellenbosch and Paarl to plant vines and make wine for sale. This market was the foundation of a major production industry which was to supply chiefly domestic needs for the next three centuries.

Although Van der Stel provided advice to these early growers, they had little capital and few skills. Moreover, a Stellenbosch or Drakenstein farmer, unlike Van der Stel who had unlimited access to the labour of Company workers, had only his own resources to rely on. And, while the Constantia farm continued to produce highly praised wines, the administration was unhelpful to other prospective wine-farmers. Without its sustained support, any reputation for quality that they might have earned was no more than fleeting. This need not have been the case; as John Barrow, private secretary to the new British governor, commented at the end of the eighteenth century '... in Drakenstein, the wine pressed from [Muscadel] is equally good, if not superior to the Constantia, though sold at one sixth of the price, of such importance is a name.'

The relative fame of Stellenbosch and Paarl as quality areas to be ranked with Constantia has come only in the twentieth century, following the establishment of major wine-trading companies in these two pioneering towns.

3

4

5

1. Rural life in the wine-farming area between Stellenbosch and Paarl. 2. Terraced houses in Stellenbosch's Herte Street were, according to tradition, built for freed slaves after emancipation in 1834. 3. Morgenhof is one of many centuries-old wine farms around Stellenbosch.

HOLLANDSCHE BIEFSTUK VERSUS ENGLISH WINE

The prosperity of Constantia during the period of Dutch rule should have been a model on which to pattern other Cape vineyards, but the Dutch East India Company discouraged the colony's farmers from becoming dependent on income from wine.

To the Company officials in Amsterdam the source of their profits was the East Indies, whereas the Cape, in the role of victualling station on the marathon voyage east or west, was no more than a necessary expense. Its sole purpose was to supply the Dutch trading vessels with provisions such as fresh meat and flour; fresh water, not wine, was required. Even Simon van der Stel, who eventually

contributed more to the Cape wine industry than any other individual, spent his first years as commander of the colony motivating wheat production. His first proclamation was '...every person who shall plant a morgen of vines shall be bound to cultivate 6 morgen with other crops...'.

Prohibition on the free trade in wine was imposed as early as 1668, when no more than ten retail licences were granted. Restrictions on retailing and heavy duties remained in force until the arrival of the British, and commentators on life at the Cape often wrote about the excessive cost of wine. Levies on alcoholic beverages were one of

the Dutch East India Company's chief sources of income at the Cape, yet wine production continued to be stifled.

There was a complete turnaround in attitude when the British administration took over in 1806 and was charged with promoting economic self-sufficiency for the colony. Cape wines were introduced to the British domestic market, entering it exempt from import tariffs, and by 1812 the English were drinking Cape wine for the first time. Sales, mostly of white wines, took off and within a few years represented 60 per cent of the Cape's export revenue.

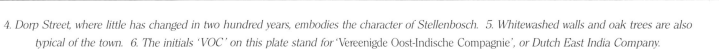

4. Dorp Street, where little has changed in two hundred years, embodies the character of Stellenbosch. 5. Whitewashed walls and oak trees are also typical of the town. 6. The initials 'VOC' on this plate stand for 'Vereenigde Oost-Indische Compagnie', or Dutch East India Company.

25

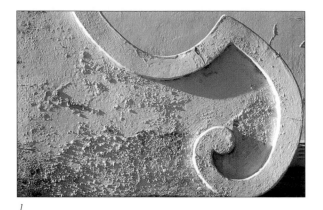

1

2

3

4

Cape Dutch farm architecture

One of the world's most distinctive styles of domestic home architecture developed around the desire of wealthy, slave-owning citizens of the Cape to demonstrate their social position. Thriving under a Dutch administration during the latter half of the eighteenth century, this newly prosperous élite for the most part was made up of farmers and traders. To them a grand house, like the ownership of slaves, was a badge of wealth, and the slaves themselves, skilled and unskilled, were employed to construct and decorate the edifice.

All the great farmhouses originally designed and built in the characteristic Cape style were erected between 1750 and 1840, and many of them during three distinct periods of prosperity. The first of these, from 1758 to 1763, resulted from the Dutch East India Company spending extravagantly with local businesses, prompted by fears of foreign invasion. The second, from 1780 to 1790, was stimulated by booming trade in Cape Town's port, when an unusual profusion of visiting merchant ships docked in the harbour en route between Europe and Asia, and even the new settlement of Australia.

The third and greatest period of wealth started with the first British occupation of the Cape in 1795, followed by a second, longer-lasting one in 1806. The new administration stimulated the Cape economy, wine-making and other industries prospered, wine-trading wholesalers set up businesses that flourished, and many impressive houses were built. Some of these were the first buildings on a virgin site and others were the grand development of an existing basic home.

The first houses the settlers built were naturally very rudimentary in design and were constructed from tree branches and a clay-based mud. As the farmers prospered they extended their homes, adding one room onto another in a row. Tree-branch walls were replaced with packed stone and mud, and as time passed extra wings were added so that the farmhouses took on the form of T-, L-, U-, H- or E-shaped structures. The walls were usually plastered and whitewashed with lime which, frequently replenished, kept rain-water from eroding the mud between the stones. Local grasses were used to thatch the roofs and inside, the ceilings were made of reeds, with a clay overlay for protection against fire. The floors were of stone, Batavian tiles or Baltic timber, and much of the furniture was crafted from local stinkwood and yellowwood. Extra buildings for stables, cowsheds, slaves' dormitories and housing for adult children were added to form a courtyard, or *werf*, around the main house.

With prosperity came a desire to improve their homes, and when the farmers set about doing so they, not unnaturally, looked back to Europe, and Holland in particular, for their

---

1. Early plasterers developed a skill for graceful work. 2. To support a central gable, a section of pitched roof had to be added at right angles to the main rooms.
3. An aerial view of Boschendal shows how the original row of rooms was extended into an H shape. 4. Gables were originally simple and at the ends
of the building. 5. Plasterwork birds above the door identify a fowl shed. 6. A highly decorative 'rococo' gable.

inspiration. Within the limitations imposed by the availability and inherent restrictions of Cape building materials and by the skills of local builders and decorators, they sought to keep up with the prevailing fashions among house designers in Europe. The shortage of architects in the colony created a demand for the use of 'house pattern' books. The customer and prospective builder could choose a basic house shape and preferred decorative features, including gables, from a book of Dutch examples, and these standard choices were then modified according to the builder's and the decorator's capabilities. In this way, Cape Dutch developed its own original look.

The gable, initially no more than the upper end wall under a pitched roof, became a focal point of Cape Dutch houses. As the local artisans proved adept at plasterwork and modelling shaped edges, the concept was adapted and became a feature of the front of the house, normally moved to the centre of the original single line of rooms, above the front door. Influenced by the trends in Holland and, to a lesser extent, those in Germany and France, the designs of these gables went through stages of fashion, from simple to baroque to rococo and finally to the more severe lines of neo-classical. The local craftsmen, too, brought design

1

2

influences from their original cultures into the creative mix. Thus one finds animist and mythical figures of Asian origin among symbols of European heritage on gables and other features.

During the final years of the Dutch East India Company's rule a Parisian architectural engineer, Louis Thibault, a German sculptor, Anton Anreith, and a German mason, Herman Schutte, arrived at the Cape. Between them they provided the designs and finishes of many gracious houses and wine cellars, including Groot Constantia, which are today classical examples of Cape Dutch architecture.

3

1. The reception room, behind the front door, was often flanked by bedrooms, left and right. 2. Decorative friezes around internal doors were a feature of most great houses. 3. Many gracious homes, such as Boschendal, featured a wide central passage where visitors were received. 4. The very best furniture was imported from Europe.

Boom and bust

'This colony can produce as excellent wine of various sorts as perhaps any country in the world.' These were the words of Sir John Cradock, the new governor of the Cape Colony who in 1811 issued a proclamation encouraging farmers to improve cultivation practices and produce quality wine for export, primarily to Britain. Nor was he the only one to recognise the potential of viticulture and the wine trade at the Cape. One of the world's first wine writers, the Englishman Cyrus Redding, described Groot Constantia and Klein Constantia as '... the most beautiful [vineyards] in the world' in his *History and description of modern wines* (1851), and goes on to say that '... [there is] no colony where a more congenial soil exists, or where better wines might be grown'.

Governor Cradock's enthusiasm was backed by practical support when Britain, waging a smouldering war against France, allowed Cape wines to be imported at very favourable tariffs, giving the Cape farmers a fighting chance against their European competitors whose transport costs were so much lower. From 1812 until 1825 the Cape was supplying 14 per cent of the British wine market, and enjoying the peak of a boom period during which vineyard owners were able to afford the lifestyle of landed gentry. The height of their prosperity was shortlived; in the summer of 1825, just as the huge 1824 harvest began to arrive in England, weather conditions in the Cape turned sour on the farmers, resulting in a failed

1. A Cape Town house, 'Saasveld', was transported to Franschhoek to house the Huguenot Museum. 2. The Berg River valley, with Paarl to the left and the Franschhoek valley entrance on the right. 3. In the Franschhoek valley, as elsewhere, vines were extensively planted during boom times, then torn out during the bust that followed.

crop that proved to be the beginning of a slow decline which developed in intensity and gravity over the next hundred years.

At the same time the British colonial government started to withdraw the economic protection it had afforded the Cape wine industry, and by 1862 all countries importing wine into Britain were paying duties levelled at one shilling a gallon. Whereas the Cape and French farmers were paying the same duty, the latter had less to pay in transport costs, and their wines, having travelled far shorter distances, arrived in better condition.

As if this were not enough, the fungal disease powdery mildew hit Cape vineyards in 1859, reducing total wine production from one million gallons to 30 000 gallons in one year. It was soon brought under control but in 1886 another pest, the phylloxera aphid which attacks a vine's roots, caused even greater havoc, laying waste vast acreages of vineyard. Following the European example, the farmers replanted their land with vines grafted onto phylloxera-resistant American rootstock, and they gradually experienced a recovery – only to face ruin again when war broke out between Boer and Briton at the end of the century.

Virtually cut off from their export markets, the farmers had no outlet for the large amounts of wine their grafted vines were now able to produce. From the end of the Anglo-Boer War

5

4. The Dutch Reformed church in Main Street, Franschhoek. 5. The entrance to La Garonne, one of the many Franschhoek farms whose name arrived with the Huguenots and has been retained to this day, contributing to the unique character of the valley.

1

2

3

4

in 1902 until 1918 the Cape government made various attempts to bring prosperity back to the wine trade. In 1905 and 1906 it made treasury grants to groups of grape growers to maintain wine production during a critical period, an initiative which led to the formation of the co-operative wineries which still play a major role in the industry today. There were cycles of boom and bust. In the good times the supply of grapes was comparatively small and merchants paid good prices; at other times, after concerted plantings of extra vineyards, the economics of over-production led to bankruptcy for many growers. Some diversified, supplementing their grape-derived income with revenue from fruit and other forms of agriculture.

In another attempt to regulate the wine industry, 1918 saw the founding of the Co-operative Winegrowers' Association of South Africa (*Koöperatiewe Wynbouersvereniging van Suid-Afrika*, or KWV). Its aim was to assist growers by providing advice, guaranteeing

1. *The hotel Grande Roche is set among vineyards at the foot of Paarl Mountain.* 2. *Paarl's valley contains a checkerboard of table grape and wine grape vineyards.* 3. *An old Paarl cellar, complete with decorative plastering, has been turned into a home.*

purchase for grapes or wine, establishing minimum price controls and setting up a unified negotiating system with wholesale customers. Its success was limited and, as the twentieth century progressed and South Africa's economic and political isolation increased, Cape grape growers found themselves supplying chiefly domestic markets with raisins, fortified wines and brandy. Although the production of fine wines began to increase in volume and importance from around 1970 – having benefited from the introduction of the cold fermentation technique in the 1950s, for example – the trade barrier of anti-apartheid sanctions ensured that South Africa's tiny domestic market remained the wine industry's only customer until 1990, when the world began to show interest in Cape wines once again.

5

6

---

4. Another historic Paarl town cellar is now a nightspot. 5. Paarl in its valley, seen from vineyards on the Simonsberg.
6. Laborie, KWV's only commercial vineyard, lies in suburban Paarl.

1

2

The major players in the industry

Founded in 1918 in response to the dire straits the Cape wine industry found itself in during the early years of this century, the *Koöperatiewe Wynbouersvereniging van Suid-Afrika*, or KWV, currently plays the most important role on the South African wine stage. This wine farmers' administrative co-operative has many functions: it owns a commercial vineyard; makes wine from purchased grapes in its huge cellars; buys wine for blending and resale; distils wine into brandy; exports wine and spirit drinks; controls all purchases and the sales of each individual wine producer; conducts research into soils, climates and varieties; and is charged with promoting the whole Cape wine production structure to every player's benefit.

Together with its affiliates, the KWV controls a major share of the sales of non-beer alcohol in South Africa. It employs a thousand people in jobs ranging from vine-grafter to chief distiller, and its headquarters sprawls over 22 hectares of land in and around the town of Paarl. Yet, since the emergence of South African wines onto the world market in the early 1990s, the role and functions of the various parts of the KWV within the local wine industry have mostly changed and are expected to continue to evolve under the influences of changing politics and the market forces of world trade.

The KWV's full name, translated as 'Co-operative Winegrowers' Association', aptly describes the body as a farmers' co-operative group, as can be found in many countries. It started out at the instigation of Charles Kohler, a wine industry leader in the early twentieth century who maintained that if the farmers grouped together to form a united front, they would be able to consolidate their bargaining powers vis-à-vis the merchants, and a realistic and stable price for their wines would result. This did not completely solve the problem

3

1. La Concordia, the head office of KWV in Paarl. 2. Oude Libertas in Stellenbosch houses the public relations operation of the Stellenbosch Farmers' Winery, including the Cape Wine Academy. 3. The Wellington valley, near Paarl, is one of many parts of the Cape winelands where vineyards are being extended.

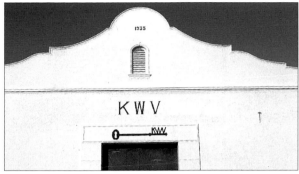

4

5

of over-production – in the period 1921 to 1923 the price per leaguer fell drastically and thousands of leaguers were poured into the Eerste River – but a precedent had been set and in 1924 the KWV was legally empowered to impose a minimum price for the farmers' distilling wine. It also guaranteed to purchase grapes and wine from the farmers, a practice which led to the stockpiling of unsold wine and the subsequent distilling of wine spirit. Today the KWV is the country's largest distiller and the watchdog over this aspect of the wine industry, exercising complete control over the volume distilled and the methods used. Its own chain of brandy distilleries provides stock for much of the large domestic market.

The guarantee to buy wine from farmers and the necessity to dispose of it caused the KWV to seek out and develop export markets. Even through the years of South Africa's economic isolation, it continued to sell small volumes of branded products as well as major stocks of wine spirit in bulk. Now able to build on long-established contacts, it is still South Africa's major wine exporter and has one of the country's largest production cellars. By local agreement, only a few of the organisation's branded products may be sold in South Africa.

In addition to marketing and distilling, the KWV offers its nearly 5000 member farmers a host of ancillary services, including viticultural and wine-making advice. It also approves all contracts between grape growers, wine producers and wholesalers, and all payments for grapes and wines have to be made through it. It even provides the manpower to administer the Wine and Spirit Board's controls over wine appellation and label content.

In addition to the KWV, there are other players in the South African wine industry whose roles are not insignificant. A small number of producing wholesalers – notably Stellenbosch

4. KWV has several satellite distilleries in outlying areas. 5. The bulk of Cape wines is made by co-operatives, some of which sell a proportion of their own wines from grand sales offices.

For my dear friends Zelmae and Phil
René Wagener
27/2/98 Boschendal.

Farmers' Winery, Distillers Corporation, Vinfruco and Douglas Green Bellingham – buy the largest percentage of the annual crop, mainly from co-operatives, and then blend wines into commercial products for local and export markets.

Most Cape wines are made in large, commercial wineries which are owned chiefly on a co-operative basis by the grape farmers themselves. These co-operatives are a legacy of the struggle to find the most economically viable means of production when the wine industry suffered the downturn that lasted from the end of last century for almost a hundred years. Today most of the wine they make is sold in bulk and reaches the public via the wholesalers, but a small proportion is bottled and sold under their own branded labels.

The largest number of labels comes from the smallest producers, a multitude of small and medium-sized estates and private cellars. Estate wineries make their wines from grapes grown on their own properties within a narrow 'terroir', or an area which has similar soils. By contrast, private wineries which are not 'estates' may buy grapes from a wider area, although in practice they tend to make their wines mainly from their own vineyards' fruit. These smaller producers concentrate on making special, more expensive wines, many of which are varietal rather than blends.

South Africa's recent re-emergence into international trade as a result of its political about-turn in the 1990s has brought about many developments in the wine industry, as in other spheres of activity. In comparison with those of other wine-producing countries, the vineyards of the Cape are large, with many properties exceeding 100 hectares. The rapid growth in export sales has brought new and dynamic forces into play, as a mature – even static – production industry now takes the opportunity to start again as new. Many cellar buildings are being erected, both as extensions of existing wineries and as totally new enterprises, the latest technology in wine-making is being implemented, and large-scale investment, in many cases by foreigners, is changing the face of this very public industry.

Changes are occurring, too, in the language of communication which, once almost exclusively Afrikaans, has become more cosmopolitan as Swiss, German, French and even Asian entrepreneurs move into the Cape winelands. And where young South African winemakers once ventured little further than the Geisenheim Wine Institute in Germany to study and gain a wider perspective, today they may be found in major wineries throughout the world. In return, South Africa has provided a base for the international corps of 'flying winemakers' who bring to this country yet another perspective on world demand.

1. These suspended red-wine fermenters at Boschendal represent considerable investment in the latest wine-making technology. 2. The oldest wine farm at the Cape, Groot Constantia, has a thoroughly modern cellar. 3. Red wine is stored in cathedral-like conditions at the KWV's enormous cellar. 4. The Cape's Sauvignon Blanc style pays homage to a Kiwi pioneer. 5. The Spier wine estate is being developed into a large complex offering entertainment, accommodation and restaurants.

The essential flavour in a wine is the taste that was in the grapes at harvest. Part of the flavour derives from the variety of the grapes, for each has its own identity, but its composition, the degree of its richness and intensity, and every little nuance of its character are rooted in the energy the vine draws from the sun and the nutrients it gathers from the soil. The specific conditions that prevail at the Cape influence the flavour of its wines – as well as that wonderfully evasive measure called quality – to a noticeable, yet incalculable, degree.

FRUITS OF THE
Earth & Sky

1

Searching for gems

Cresting hills, resting on valley floors or majestically sited below mountain peaks, Cape vineyards may be found in a wide array of locations within a few minutes' drive. It has not always been so; the early settlers planted their vineyards on low-lying land that could easily be cultivated. Many of the first grants of Cape land consisted of a single block containing the homestead portion on the lower, more level land where crops and vines were grown; the middle slopes where stock grazed; and an unfarmed section of the wild mountain behind.

Centuries later the valleys and lower slopes still bear large tracts of vines, but on some of the farms the indigenous vegetation has been cleared from the higher mountainsides and farmers, with a better understanding of the vines' requirements for good drainage and cooler temperatures, have extended their plantings upward. As an example, at Klein Constantia there is a gradient of more than 250 metres between the lowest-altitude vineyards − from

2

1. Vineyards advance up the slopes of the Helderberg, which are home to more than a dozen wine cellars.

2. In the Tulbagh valley, vines are grown only at its western edge where the rainfall is highest.

3

4

which the great sweet wines of past centuries were made – and the highest, where Chardonnay and Sauvignon Blanc vines have recently been planted.

The varied terrain of the Cape, particularly of its southwestern corner, offers farmers a wide range of locations, microclimates and soils in which to grow the different varieties of grapes that produce fine wines. Vineyards may be located between 50 metres above sea-level near the coast and altitudes of about 1000 metres in the mountains, and within this range the chief factor influencing the choice of the site itself is the availability of sufficient moisture to keep the vine healthy all year round. At the same time, the drainage must be adequate, as too much water around the plant's roots is as bad as too little.

The choice of grape variety to be grown in a certain site depends to a large extent on the composition of that site's soil and the temperatures it experiences during the growing and ripening seasons. When a new variety is incorporated into a planting programme the farmer will also consider which varieties thrive in adjacent vineyards, reaping the benefits of his own experience and that of his neighbours and predecessors. In some areas of the Cape consistently superior wines of a certain style have been produced for long enough to influence the planning of future vineyards. Moreover, extensive scientific research is being carried out to establish which varieties grow best in certain conditions and the information gleaned from such research also helps the farmer to select the variety best suited to the ground he has at his disposal.

Cape grape growers are fortunate in that there are no regulations restricting their choice of varieties to cultivate and, like their New World counterparts, they can plant the vines that are most likely to give them the best return. As the world markets show an increased preference for dry wines, Chardonnay, Sauvignon Blanc, Cabernet Sauvignon, Shiraz and Merlot are becoming as popular in the vineyards of the Cape as they are in other developing wine-producing countries. In addition, the Cape can boast Pinotage, a hybrid between Cinsaut and Pinot Noir which was bred in South Africa more than 50 years ago. This unique variety brings another degree of colour and fruit flavour to the spectrum of local red wines.

3. In the isolated McGregor valley, south of Robertson, indigenous fynbos grows in limestone-rich soil alongside irrigated vineyards.

4. Permanent irrigation piping has been installed in a low-rainfall vineyard in the Breede River valley.

1

2

3

The fashions of the market

The wine grape, *Vitis vinifera*, has many thousands of varieties, but only a few produce the wines that are popular among the world's consumers. In South Africa only about ten of these are being regularly planted in the annual programmes in which Cape vineyards are being renewed, and they belong to the group of varieties made fashionable throughout the world by the French wine culture. Even Pinotage, the Cape's only home-grown variety, is a hybrid cross of two French ones, Pinot Noir and Cinsaut.

The most fashionable varieties have been popularised by the international wine trade, and growers everywhere have been encouraged to plant Chardonnay and Cabernet Sauvignon – the grapes used in France's classic wines of Burgundy and Bordeaux – in preference to varieties that are less easy to sell to the regular wine drinker. This is the pattern followed in all the New World wine-producing regions, including in South Africa. Local farmer Danie de Wet, a pioneer of large-scale planting of premium white wines, has had an evangelical influence on the planting of Chardonnay vines in the lime-rich soils of the Robertson region, where every plant depends for survival on being regularly showered with irrigation water from the Breede River throughout the year. Today his farm, Dewetshof, and his neighbours' farms may well represent South Africa's leading Chardonnay district.

Although outwardly very similar, the grapes of different varieties have recognisably different flavours which are still identifiable in the juice after the sugar has been removed. It is these flavours that distinguish a Pinotage wine, for example, as a Pinotage wherever in the world it may be produced, although the nuances added by soil and climate determine different styles. The soils at the Cape are undoubtedly unique, but in addition to these the moderating of potentially high temperatures by the southeasterly wind, together with the remarkable degree of sunlight intensity that falls on the vineyards, contribute to the style that is distinguished as 'Cape'.

4

1. Sauvignon Blanc in Constantia vineyards. 2. Danie de Wet pioneered growing Chardonnay in the Robertson area. 3. The farm Jordan's varietal mix is typical of a Cape vineyard: Chardonnay to left and right, Sauvignon Blanc in the foreground, Cabernet Sauvignon at the back, and Merlot and Pinot Noir in the centre.

The following varieties are those most commonly planted in Cape vineyards, and they are used to make both varietal wines and blends. Chenin Blanc, the most widely planted variety in South Africa, is used to make many different styles of wine. Traditionally the 'workhorse' in both vineyard and cellar, it makes dry whites for general quaffing as well as noble sweet wines, and it is a base for sparkling wines and raw material for brandy distillation. Its richest flavours are produced when the vine is restricted in growth and production, and it rewards cultivation as a bush vine with a noticeably fruity character. Wines made from Chenin Blanc grapes gain an extra dimension if they are fermented in barrels.

Chardonnay is undoubtedly the most versatile of all varieties, white or red. When the grapes ripen fully they have a rich flavour whether grown in warm or cool conditions, with or without irrigation, in soils that are rich in clay or in lime. They are grown successfully in every wine-producing region of the Cape, and have been made into award-winning wines in almost every one of them. Given that the grapes are grown in a healthy vineyard, the structure of the wine and the intensity of its flavour depend chiefly on the size of the crop: with fewer grapes per vine, the flavour intensifies. When fermented in a sealed tank, Chardonnay

4. It has been discovered that Colombard grapes, originally planted to make brandy, also produce aromatic, fruity white wine under Cape conditions. 5. The slopes of the Helderberg, overlooking False Bay, are excellent for Chardonnay.

can give luscious tropical fruit flavours, or it extracts delicious supplementary flavours from yeast and wood when fermented in oak barrels. Like any other wine, its flavour can be varied depending on whether it is fermented at a relatively high temperature or at a low one when the yeast action is slow, but in the case of Chardonnay there is a greater likelihood of success with multiple variations in the procedure. In addition to producing dry white wine, Chardonnay grapes are used in some of the base wines from which sparkling wine is made, in South Africa by the *cap classique* method. Although they have to be picked when not fully ripe, and the flavour at first is somewhat restrained, it develops later to enrich the bottle-fermented product.

The Sauvignon Blanc variety exemplifies perfectly the maxim that wine is made in the vineyard, since the flavour in the grape on the vine carries right through to the eventual wine. The best Sauvignon Blanc wines are fresh and lean, with either a grassy or a tropical fruit style, but only certain vineyards under informed care can produce these intense flavours. Some Cape producers have made a name for the excellence and character of their Sauvignon Blancs, but others have still to find the secret.

Cape Riesling, correctly known as Crouchen Blanc, originated in southern France but is now seldom grown there. It is widely grown in the Cape, though, and produces a lightly flavoured, crisply structured white wine that makes a refreshing alfresco drink in South Africa's warm summer weather. Even though this variety may not be sold outside South Africa as a Riesling, its popularity in the domestic market has hampered efforts to correct the error of its name.

Riesling is the great white-wine grape from Germany, although it is currently at the bottom of a downturn in the world's popularity poll and is not grown widely in South Africa. Known here as Weisser Riesling or Rhine Riesling in an attempt to reduce the confusion with Cape Riesling, it has spicy, peppery flavours and can be made into quality dry and sweet wines that have long ageing potential.

1. One of the few Cape cellars to specialise in Shiraz (foreground), Bellingham is also one of the country's leading exporters. 2. The Souzão grape variety, used mainly for port, is one of only two that have naturally red juice. The other is Pontac. 3. Cabernet Sauvignon grapes, somewhat short of peak ripeness.

4

5

6

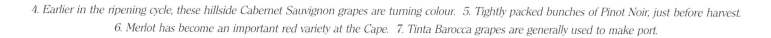

7

Colombard grapes go into most of South Africa's dry white wines at the modest end of the price scale. This variety was originally planted at the Cape especially for brandy production, but it caused surprise when wine-makers found that it produced a remarkably fragrant and agreeably fruity table wine, with more character than it has shown elsewhere, chiefly in Europe and the United States. It tends to lose this appeal with age and, as a rule, should be drunk within a year of harvest.

A hundred years ago Sémillon was virtually the only grape variety grown in the Cape. Today it is a minor player, its broad, rich and comparatively neutral flavours having been superseded by the more pronounced character of Chardonnay and Sauvignon Blanc. Nevertheless, the variety is due to make a challenge, as it is flexible, makes excellent wines in many areas, and responds well to being fermented in oak. Some Cape cellars are already producing fine Sémillon wines.

Bukettraube is a hybrid of German origin which has comparatively high acid content at full ripeness and is suited to making semi-sweet wines. As these were traditionally the most popular wines in the domestic South African market, it was widely planted in the Cape. It is now only a minor player and its popularity is declining.

Cabernet Sauvignon is the grape that gave the red wines of Bordeaux their unmatched reputation for consistency and excellence. Although often lacking in richness, the wine has a distinctly individual flavour that allows even the novice wine drinker to recognise it. It acquires from the grape skins a firm tannin structure which softens over time, benefiting from the slow, controlled oxidation that occurs in an oak barrel. Traditionally, Cabernet Sauvignon vines have been grown in unirrigated vineyards near the coast, but more recently this variety has been spearheading the expansion of red grape varieties into inland areas dependent on irrigation.

Merlot vines were originally planted to provide a blending partner for Cabernet Sauvignon, but on their own have produced some of South Africa's best red wines. They have settled well into the Cape, and several areas that are traditionally planted with red wine varieties are showing greater affinity for Merlot than they do for its more famous partner.

Pinotage is the Cape's own variety, hybridised from Pinot Noir and Cinsaut. The grapes have thick, richly pigmented skins and produce an intensely coloured and boldly flavoured wine that benefits from oak maturation. Pinotage vines are grown most successfully as untrellised bush vines, with the best grapes coming from comparatively small plants which produce tiny crops. The vineyards are usually situated near the coast and are not irrigated.

Shiraz vines thrive in the warm growing and ripening conditions of the Cape vineyards, producing a fruity, deep red wine under almost all conditions. The wine is supple and combines well with oak flavours.

Never a glamorous variety, Cinsaut was traditionally grown in South Africa to make large volumes of inexpensive, early maturing red wine. It went through a decline in domestic popularity at the end of the 1980s and was replaced in many vineyards, but the current export demand for Cape red wines has given it a new, although possibly temporary, lease of life. The grapes have a soft, fragile skin which contributes comparatively little flavour or tannin to the sweetish character derived from the juice.

Pinot Noir, the great red grape from Burgundy, is as unsettled at the Cape as it is elsewhere in the New World, but when given special care it can produce some notable wines. A number of South African wine-makers are dedicating their careers to extracting fine red wines from Pinot Noir. A large proportion of the grapes also go into a richly flavoured white wine that forms the base for sparkling wine made by the *cap classique* method.

4. *Earlier in the ripening cycle, these hillside Cabernet Sauvignon grapes are turning colour.* 5. *Tightly packed bunches of Pinot Noir, just before harvest.*
6. *Merlot has become an important red variety at the Cape.* 7. *Tinta Barocca grapes are generally used to make port.*

The mermaid in the vineyard

Vines reproduce easily from cuttings, and whatever variety a wine-farmer may choose to grow, he plants a new vineyard from cuttings, never seed. Thus every Cabernet Sauvignon vine in any Cape vineyard is a part of one original Cabernet Sauvignon vine from Europe. Although all vines of a certain variety share the same genetics, being all descended from the same plant, they are not absolutely identical, and cuttings are taken only from vines which exhibit desirable features, such as small bunches or a leafy canopy.

Planting a new vineyard is not as simple a procedure as merely planting cuttings and allowing them to mature into grape-bearing vines. Since a phylloxera epidemic swept through many of the world's vineyards in the latter half of the nineteenth century, and as no

1. After young vines have been pruned, the cut ends of the branches are sealed. 2. At the beginning of winter, the vine's extravagant summer growth is cut back. 3. Grafted vines which have developed tiny roots and buds are sorted in the nursery.

3

4

5

effective chemical control for the aphid that attacks the vine's roots has yet been developed, almost all wine-grape vines in the world are a grafted combination of two plants.

The top half, or head, with the branches, leaves and grapes, is a *Vitis vinifera* vine of one or other variety, and the lower half, from the stem down and including the complete root section, belongs to a different species that is resistant to phylloxera and originates in North America. This latter vine type, destined to provide only the below-ground, rooted section of all vineyards, is cultivated *en masse* to provide a source of root material for grafting.

During the winter period of dormancy, the best scion (i.e. grape-bearing vine) cuttings are selected and pruned from living vines in, for example, an existing Chardonnay vineyard, and shoots are pruned from a rootstock plantation. The Chardonnay cane and the rootstock cuttings are grafted together, one by one, usually indoors. Once they have formed a bond, the new vines are planted in nursery soil side by side in long rows, where they remain until they have had a chance to form roots.

The stripling vine, with its tiny, hair-like root system, is planted out in the new Chardonnay vineyard about a metre from each neighbour in rows about 2.5 metres apart. This creates a vineyard population of approximately 3500 vines per hectare. Some growers have experimented with high-density plantings of as many as 11 000 vines per hectare, but it is not yet clear whether significant differences are created by the lower yield expected from each vine under such conditions.

Vines may also be grafted in the field, in which case the rootstock stem is planted and the cutting of the interface is carried out on site. The stems are grafted and bound with the rootstock established in the soil.

A variation on the standard grafting technique is called aerial grafting. Thin sections of rootstock are planted and these bud normally in spring. Then the rootstock is grafted with a bud from a chosen variety.

6

4. A bud has been grafted onto a growing vine. 5. Scion cuttings are trimmed to the required size before being grafted onto rootstock cuttings.
6. The previous year's growth is pruned back to leave only enough for the following year's small crop.

47

The annual cycle of growth

For vines growing in the Cape the year begins in the spring month of September, when the first green buds break out of the plant's winter bark. From these fingernail-sized buds green leaves and tiny stems unfurl, pushing towards the sky. By October lush green vegetation covers the vine, and small clusters of minute flowers appear on the fruit-bearing branches. In the course of the month the flowers are fertilised and the clusters develop into the shape of grape bunches, with green fruits the size of a pin-head.

Through November and December shoots continue to sprout and the plant maintains its energetic growth. If this becomes too strong and creates an imbalance between vegetation and crop, shoots are removed by topping. In a less vigorous vineyard, only the tips of the shoots are cut off. By the end of December the grapes will have grown almost to full size and the skins of some red varieties start changing colour from green to red.

By the turn of the year summer is fast approaching its full strength, and January skies are normally clear and blue. The vines receive long hours of direct exposure to the sun, and the grapes of the early-ripening varieties are nearing full maturity. As February progresses most varieties are ripening towards their peak, and the plants are trimmed to a hedge shape to allow maximum sunlight to reach the bunches. This is a critical time for the wine-maker, who assesses the readiness of the grapes for picking by their appearance and their taste, as well as in the laboratory. As soon as he judges the fruit to be at the ultimate point of ripeness, the harvesting begins. It continues through March, and as it does so the leaves of later-ripening varieties are selectively plucked so that grapes still on the vine can reap maximum benefit from the sun, increasing their sugar content and advancing towards ripeness. Those left to the very end of the harvest season, in April, are richly sweet and will be made into late harvest wines.

As autumn arrives the vine's leaves change colour, turning to yellow and orange. May sees the falling of the leaves and the first bare stems. Many of those representing the previous year's growth are clipped back in the course of pruning. By June the vines are dormant and the full pruning programme is under way. In the following weeks young vines are trained on the trellis and new ones are planted. Rain, sometimes torrential, comes to the Cape in June, July and August, soaking the vineyards and filling the dams. By the time long spells of sunshine, weak at first, return in September, the cycle of growth begins once more.

1

2

3

4

5

6

1. A Boschendal vineyard in winter. The oaks feel spring already, but the vines are slow to waken. 2. Sunshine lights up a young vineyard bursting into spring growth. 3. Branches, leaves and even grape bunches will develop from these buds. 4. In the Hex River valley, renowned for its table grapes, full summer produces a patchwork of colour. 5. Within a month the young shoots of these vines will reach the tops of the poles. 6. The yearly clock returns to winter, with bare rows of vines.

1

Cultivating the vineyards

Two elements that are essential to the healthy growth of vines are nutritional soil space in which the wide-ranging root systems can develop, and access to moisture in the most parched of dry seasons, year after year. Where winter rainfall is both regular and sufficient, the layer of clay under the nutrient soil provides a reservoir of water for summer. In the Cape's semi-arid growing areas irrigation water regularly sprayed into the vineyards fulfills the same role. In both cases, when a new vineyard is being prepared, the land is ripped and ploughed to the likely full depth of the roots, with rocks and earth being shaken loose to allow air and plant roots to penetrate the soil easily. Without this deep ripping of often heavily compacted soil, the growth and crop potential of the planted vine tend to be stunted.

Samples of the soil are analysed to determine whether the mineral and nutritional composition should be improved before planting takes place. Most Cape soils are acidic, and

2

3

4

1. Plastic sheeting is used to reduce evaporation from around the newly planted vine's roots during summer. 2. A protective layer of plastic is used in the nursery too, and grafted vine stalks are planted through holes in it. 3. At the end of summer, excess growth is clipped from the vines.

5

6

additional lime often has to be ploughed into the topsoil. In winter young vines are planted as grafted sections of vine stem with a small established root structure. They bud and begin to develop stem and leaf growth in spring, and by the end of summer have to be pruned, like more mature plants. In fact, vineyard management during the vines' first years is almost the same as that for producing vines. The young vines are susceptible to the same pests and diseases, and need a similar spraying programme to protect them and enhance healthy growth. Weeds sprouting between the vines must be controlled, as if they are allowed to develop they utilise nutrition and moisture otherwise meant for vineyard sustenance. In winter, nitrogen-enhancing vegetation such as rye or oats is grown between the rows to improve the soil environment. These crops are cut down before the vines' spring shoots develop so that they do not compete.

4. Ploughing late-summer weeds between the rows provides a welcome meal for the egrets. 5. In preparing a future vineyard, organic material is added to the soil mix. 6. Once the topsoil has been loosened, plastic sheeting is laid down and the young vines are planted.

51

1

2

3

Vines are naturally crawling plants and if left to their own devices would form low, horizontal bushes. In order that the grapes may develop in the shade of the leaves, and to facilitate harvesting by two-legged humans, wine-grape vines are trained and tied to grow into a goblet shape, known as a bush vine. Alternatively, they may be attached to rows of wire strung between poles, a system known as trellising. Both these techniques are used in the Cape, and both also provide support for the heavily laden vines, keeping the grapes off the ground. Trellising appears to be linked to regions rather than varieties, and is used throughout semi-arid areas such as Vredendal and Robertson where it allows a uniform degree of irrigation to give even growth and bunch development. Bush vines, found in many unirrigated growing areas, are also virtually standard in some drier regions such as Darling.

Given a standard size of vine, and assuming that all other variables are equal, the larger the number of grapes the plant has to develop and ripen, the more diluted is the flavour. There is only so much nutrition available to the plant from the soil around its roots, and this has to supply not only all the plant's cells, but also the stressful demands of the burgeoning crop of grapes. The size of the producing part of the vine, the root structure, the stem and branches, and the canopy of leaves all need to be in balance with the size of the crop of grapes that have to be ripened. To improve this balance in a vineyard where the fertility of the soil or genetic factors may cause a vine to grow excessive amounts of wood, leaf or grape material, a skilful vineyard manager can trim excess plant growth or excess crop from the vine.

In addition, some grape varieties ripen more readily when they are mildly exposed to direct sunlight, and the crop from these vines benefits from a percentage of the sun-facing leaves

4

1. Overhead sprinklers supply moisture to a trellised vineyard in early summer. 2. Mechanical pruning in early summer reduces excess foliage and gives the ripening grape bunches access to sunlight. 3. Vines are susceptible to mildew diseases at flowering, and preventative spraying is essential.

being plucked away by hand. If excess crop is to be trimmed from the vine, the bunches should be removed long before they become ripe, whereas if leaves are to be plucked this should be done nearer to the harvesting date.

Only when a vine is supremely healthy and well supplied with water can it fully ripen its burden of grapes, so fading water reserves in many Cape soils during the long, dry summer were historically a handicap to the expansion of vineyards. Before the winter rainfall was harnessed into dams, allowing regular summer irrigation in the majority of Cape vineyards, South Africa's wine-growing areas were limited to within a hundred kilometres of the coast. Now, more than 50 per cent of all South Africa's wines are made from the fruit of vines grown under permanent and regular irrigation.

4. Weeding the vineyard lessens the competition for nutrients the young vines face. 5. In midsummer, as the vineyard's crop ripens, further protection against mildew diseases is necessary. 6. These newly budded vines will soon be rid of the winter growth around their bases.

1

Labour on the Cape's wine farms

Unlike in many other wine-producing regions of the world, the work in a Western Cape winery is highly labour-intensive. Most of the Cape farms are large, and the labourers' community on each one is more like a village than it is elsewhere. For more than three centuries many have been the residential base for at least a dozen families, some of which have made their home on a particular farm for generation after generation.

For most of the history of European settlement at the Cape the farmer and his family had a paternalistic relationship with his employees and their families. He provided accommodation and the workers laboured as their part of the bargain. Only during the last quarter of

2

1. The row of houses (mid-foreground) provided for the workers on this wine farm is an example of improving conditions for Cape farm communities. 2. Most larger Cape farms today have crèches providing community child care.

the twentieth century have conditions and attitudes begun to change, both in the labourers' cottages and in their workplace.

In 1982 a group of Stellenbosch farmers and sociologists from Stellenbosch University formed an organisation called the Rural Foundation. At that time, many labourers' cottages were being upgraded and provided with services such as electricity, but the social fabric of the communities remained threadbare. The education level among their members was low, and there were no health care services, nor sporting or cultural facilities to enrich their lives. With the objective of motivating farm workers to take charge of their own upliftment, the Rural Foundation was designed to offer farmers the means to improve conditions for their workers and enable each community to generate changes from within. Once both a farmer and the community resident on his farm had volunteered to participate in the scheme, a developer trained in sociology was appointed to act as co-ordinator.

Unlike previous assistance schemes, the Rural Foundation's training was intended to help the farmer as much as the workers. While the former erected buildings for health clinics and crèches, members of the community elected and maintained committees to operate them, and basic nursing and crèche management skills were taught to selected farm residents. Fields were cleared for sports activities and the communities organised competitive leagues.

The programme was so successful that within a short time there were more than 80 farm communities on the waiting list to be allocated co-ordinators. Nor was it confined to the Western Cape: it quickly spread to the rest of rural South Africa, and today involves approximately 80 per cent of South Africa's total farm-working population. The natural dissemination of skills, a general broadening of awareness, and the clear-cut economic benefits of a healthy and happier workforce have all contributed to its success.

DOPS AND TOTS

The practice of paying vineyard labourers in kind has occurred to some extent and at some time or other in every wine-producing region. On the Cape estates of the eighteenth century, the slaves were rewarded with brandy and wine which were usually issued several times a day. Not surprisingly, the peace of the countryside was often interrupted by rowdy behaviour, and the land-owners would debate the wisdom of a system that used liquor as wages. However, they feared losing valued and scarcely replaceable workers, so the system remained in place, continuing as a general practice until it was declared illegal in the 1970s. The labourer would receive a 'dop' before he began work, several more at evenly spaced intervals during the day, and a double ration in the evening.

Historically, the farmer preferred to dispense brandy rather than wine, as it could be stored for longer and he did not have to pay excise duty on the brandy made for his staff. When the KWV took control of distilling, farm stills were outlawed and the co-operative agreed to supply farmers with cheap wine for their labourers instead.

During, and since, the apartheid years, the 'dop' system has been highlighted as an example of worker exploitation in South Africa. However, economic and practical issues have been more effective than political pressure in eliminating what became an ultimately counter-productive method of rewarding and retaining staff.

3

---

3. Lunch break during harvest. Picking grapes is a labour-intensive activity in the Cape, and at this busy time of year additional labour is often drafted in, but the bulk of the work is still done by the farm's own staff.

Late summer in the wine-growing regions of the Cape is a season of intense activity, the climax of the wine-farmer's labours. In the southern hemisphere the first quarter of the calendar year is when the vineyards' harvest is gathered, when the wine-makers prepare themselves and their cellars for the practising of their art. From January through to the end of March each year, rumbling convoys of trucks and trailers piled high with grapes, a powerful scent of ripeness hanging in the air, and the rich and colourful humour of thousands of vineyard workers dominate the winelands.

THE CAPE AT

Harvest Time

1

The harvesting pattern

Ask any Cape wine-maker what is the most crucial decision he must make when creating a fine wine, and most will cite judging the exact point at which the grapes are ready for picking. The juice of a fully ripe wine grape is sweeter than that of a table grape, containing almost 25 per cent sugar. At the same point, its flavours have reached the peak of their development. Full ripeness is essential for making a rich, flavourful wine, and as the summer progresses, the wine-maker spends more and more time in the vineyard, tasting the grapes and measuring the sweetness of the crop of each variety before he chooses the ideal time for harvesting each

2

1. Even though they are of the same variety, grapes growing in the granite-based loam on the slope will only be ready for harvesting some time after the grapes grown in the sandy soil of the valley bottom have ripened. 2. Holidays at harvest time mean sweet fruit and vineyard adventures.

individual vineyard block. Once he has made his decision, the pickers move in, working at speed to ensure that the grapes arrive at the cellar in ultimate condition. Although more and more mechanised vine harvesters are being seen in the Cape vineyards, they are still used less for stripping the vines of their fruit than in other wine-producing regions of the world. Here grape harvesting is still a labour-intensive operation, and in the summer months the vineyards are a colourful hive of activity, with additional labour often being called in from other areas to supplement the year-round vineyard workers. Most grape bunches are still cut from the vine by hand, placed in lug-boxes and then transferred to a large bin on a farm trailer or the back of a truck.

Grapes ripen unevenly across the expanse of a single vineyard, affected by changing soil structure or availability of moisture under the rows of vines. Harvesting teams often pick the ripe grapes of one variety in one section of a vineyard block, then move to another vineyard, leaving the rest of the original vineyard's crop to gain sweetness. In mid-summer, when several varieties reach peak ripeness at the same time, the teams spend the full day cutting and collecting bunches. This could mean spending as many as 12 hours in the field, a long stretch that is generally relieved by three meal breaks. To beat the intensity of the midday heat, the harvesters' day starts early; in the vineyards before dawn, they must be ready to begin cutting as soon as the rising sun gives them enough light.

The sun is already well in the sky by the time a bin is full, and the grapes are transported to the cellar without delay. Not all farms have their own wine-making operations and a large number of growers deliver their crops to a central fermentation cellar. Seventy co-operative cellars crush more than 80 per cent of the total South African harvest. Tractor-drawn trailers full of grapes are a common sight in the winelands during the hot summer months, and their snail's pace is often a test of patience for other road-users.

It is fortunate for the farmers that not all the grape varieties ripen at the same time. Chardonnay grapes, for example, have already started to gain sweetness when many

3

4

3. Grapes carried in lug-boxes are less likely to be prematurely crushed than those tipped directly into a bin. These boxes are awaiting the wine-maker's decision to pick. 4. A fully ripe vineyard can be picked more quickly by machine than by hand.

1

3

2

Cabernet Sauvignon ones are just turning from green to red and are still a month away from maturity. The different varieties ripen to a fairly predictable pattern, and this allows the wine-maker to plan his cellar work so that each one may be harvested when fully ripe and then slotted into his production line. Sauvignon Blanc, Pinot Noir, Pinotage and Merlot, for example, are early-ripening varieties, whereas Cinsaut, Riesling and Cabernet Sauvignon are normally picked some two or three weeks later. But there are other factors which the wine-maker must also take into account when planning the schedule for his cellar. The air temperature when the grapes are ripening, the altitude of the vineyard, the size of the crop and the health of the vines all affect the speed of ripening and thus play a role in determining the calendar date of harvesting.

The first grapes to be picked for wine-making each year are generally slightly under-ripe Chardonnay and Pinot Noir which are destined to become sparkling wine by the *cap classique* method. These specially chosen grapes begin to arrive at the cellars in late January, and from then on there is a steady stream of arrivals until the end of March, when the last of the late varieties and small batches of extra-sweet grapes selected for dessert wines are delivered. By the end of the harvesting season autumn is just beginning at the Cape. In comparison, other wine-growing regions in the southern hemisphere are usually only midway through their season. In Chile and New Zealand for example, where vineyards are much further south than at the Cape, the clouds of early winter are scudding across the sky when grapes are still being brought in.

4

1. Lug-boxes are used chiefly for collecting grapes which are to be used in speciality wines such as cap classique sparkling wine.
2. The pickers wash sticky juice off their hands before they take a meal break.

3. *Bunches of red grapes are dumped, uncrushed, straight into the press.* 4. *In most vineyards, picking begins early in the day and when breakfast time comes round the shadows are still long.*

Reversing the clock

Most wine-growing areas around the world have spells of intensely hot weather during mid- and late summer, and the Cape is no exception. Particularly in mountain-enclosed basins such as the Tulbagh, Paarl, Franschhoek and Worcester valleys, temperatures can become scorching, and when grapes harvested on an excessively hot day are crushed, the resulting juice would normally enter the fermentation cycle at a high temperature. As warm grape juice quickly loses its precious aroma and flavour content, most production cellars use chilling facilities to reduce the temperature of juice extracted from grapes brought in from the vineyards on especially hot days.

The juice from grapes picked under cooler conditions requires less emergency care, and two Cape wine estates have pioneered harvesting grapes during the night hours, when temperatures are at their lowest in the 24-hour daily cycle. At Twee Jonge Gezellen in the

1. In the middle of the night, lamps are required to find the bunches and cut them free from the vine. 2. The Twee Jonge Gezellen estate harvests more than 100 hectares of vineyard at night, all by hand.

SHAKING THE GRAPES
FROM THE VINE

Mechanical harvesters can operate by night or day, removing the grapes from the vine as effectively during the hours of darkness as during daylight. Although this form of harvesting is less popular in the Cape than it is in Australia, New Zealand and many of the European wine-making countries, on some farms the huge machines can be seen making their way along the rows of vines at any time of day or night.

Whereas the picking of grapes by hand is a comparatively careful operation in which whole bunches are clipped off the vine stems, harvesting mechanically is less precise. The tractor-like machine straddles a trellised row and a co-ordinated group of paddles shakes the vine on both sides, removing the grapes from their hold. A pneumatic blower blasts air through the grape skins and juice as they fall into a collecting hopper at the base of the harvester, and any leaf material is blown away before it can fall into the bottom of the bin with the liquid contents of the grape. When the hopper is full, the liquid is transferred to a bin on a tractor-drawn trailer or the back of a truck.

Tulbagh valley and at L'Ormarins near Franschhoek, grapes are picked by the light of battery-powered lamps and the moon.

For two months every year the entire staff of Twee Jonge Gezellen, numbering more than a hundred people, wake in the late afternoon, breakfast, and then head off into the vineyards or into the cellar to work as the twilight fades. Throughout the night they go through the stages of the vineyard-to-cellar cycle, cutting the ripe bunches from the vines, transporting the grapes to the cellar, operating the crushing machinery and setting the fermentation process in motion. When the sun rises over the Witzenberg Mountains above Tulbagh, it shines on the Twee Jonge Gezellen team heading for home, supper and a good day's sleep.

3

4

5

3. As dawn breaks over the Tulbagh valley, the last bunches are picked before the vineyard team will head for home. 4. The objective is to bring all the grapes into the cellar during the coolest part of the daily cycle. 5. The cellar work, too, goes on all night, to ensure that the grapes and juice remain cool while being processed.

Squeezing grape juice

Once the bin of grapes arrives at the cellar, it is assessed for value and then follows a selected course of treatment. In almost all the larger cellars the load is weighed before being crushed. The grower's return is normally determined by the average sugar content of the load, its weight and the desirability of the grape variety.

At some cellars sulphur is added to the grapes as a juice preservative before they are crushed, and at many the juice is chilled immediately after extraction. The larger cellars have fully mechanised handling systems at the grape arrival point, and some are geared to handle the collection and processing of over a thousand tons of grapes in a 24-hour period. At the height of harvesting, the cellar staff work a shift system to crush, chill, cold-macerate and drain grapes and juice continuously until the pressure of grapes arriving at the cellar relaxes.

Truck-loads of grapes seldom arrive after dark, but a dramatically busy day will see the sun set on queues of laden vehicles waiting to off-load. Every batch has to receive the standard treatment in preparation for fermentation, and the cellar will be busy late into the night.

There are certain advantages to size. In a larger cellar, wines of one variety from different vineyards can be made separately and in different styles. Moreover, the natural influences on quality that vary from season to season – like rain, wind and temperature – conspire to have a different effect on each vineyard, vintage by vintage. Thus as the quality of grapes from the same vineyard differs from one year to the next, each year a major cellar can benefit from being able to select the crops of several vineyards to obtain the best results.

On a smaller scale, most Cape estates and private wineries have several vineyards of each of the major grape varieties, growing on different soil and under varying conditions, even though they may be relatively close to one another. Some wine-makers choose to blend the grapes of completely contrasting vineyards, whereas others keep separate the different batches of one variety all the way from vineyard to bottling and provide each with unique packaging, enabling the customer to compare the different styles and select his preference.

1

2

3

4

1. In a small cellar operation it is relatively easy to give individual attention to small volumes of grapes from particular vineyard blocks.
2. A mechanical screw pushes grape bunches into the crusher where the stems are removed.

5

A small operation also has the opportunity to better manage the interface between vineyard and cellar, determining optimum harvesting dates and crop sizes, and to give individual treatment to small volumes of special quality.

Selecting grapes by hand is a time-honoured first step in achieving quality. At very small cellars, such as Nitída in Durbanville and Grangehurst in Stellenbosch, comparatively few grapes arrive each harvesting day, and by painstakingly grading the grapes the wine-maker can separate the marvellous from the mediocre. At larger operations careful planning in the design of the cellar affords him a similar opportunity. At Vergelegen, in Somerset West's Lourensford valley, every grape bunch is carried to the cellar in a small case load and inspected and graded on a moving belt between arrival and pressing.

Grapes for subtly flavoured wines also require special treatment, particularly those for *cap classique* sparkling wines which require juice without skin character. A computerised grape press can squeeze the berries so gently that when the skin breaks, the juice flows freely without taking flavour or colour from the skin. When wines are to be made using this type of juice treatment, the grape bunches are collected and brought to the cellar in small crates, then dumped straight into the press with skins unbroken.

3. At a large co-operative, truck-loads of grapes are weighed before being tipped into the receiving bin. 4. On a hot summer's day, a procession of grape transporters await their turn at the receiving bin. 5. The biggest co-operative cellars are able to handle thousands of tons of grapes per day.

Wine-making is a creative process in which certain principles of chemistry and physics are harnessed by an ingenious hand to transform the sweet juice of grapes into an array of alcoholic beverages. Although these beverages can all be described as wine, they vary greatly in colour, density and flavour, according to the effects of nature and the wine-maker's ideals and objectives. The routes the wine-makers take to achieve their objectives are as diverse as their personalities, and the results offer the consumer an endless variety of wines to enjoy. In the following pages a small selection of the Cape's most respected wine-makers explain how they realise their goals.

MAKING

Cape Wines

1

Glimpses into some Cape cellars

Wine cellars are like signatures; no two are alike. The cellar-master's requirements are so individual that the size and composition of each one's domain are unique. The only factor common to all cellars is the need to protect the flavour that the soil and the environment have given to the grape, and to reproduce it in the wine. This need drives all choices related to the location of the cellar, its size and its accessibility. In the vineyard, retaining all the desired qualities of the grape in the eventual wine is the factor which determines the number of grapes that are allowed to ripen on each vine and the date or hour of harvesting each block. The same factor plays a vital role in the design and construction of a cellar, determining its scale and format.

Many cellars handle the complete wine-making process, from pressing the grapes as they arrive to labelling the bottles of wine. Others are equipped only for pressing the grapes and fermenting the juice, as it was a common practice in the past for farmers merely to proceed so far and then send the resulting wine to a wholesaler to be blended and matured.

2

1. Cordoba is an example of a small, modern winery at the Cape. 2. Its cellar is built into the mountain slope, so that juice and wine can flow from higher to lower levels by gravity. 3. After having been rinsed, used barrels are prepared for the next vintage.

3

4

Among those cellars that do make their own wine, some are tiny, barely larger than a double garage, whereas others may cover a hectare. Whatever its extent, when a cellar is being planned there are two basic rules to be borne in mind. The first is that there should be a natural progression from the arrival of the grapes through the stages of juice processing, fermentation and maturation to the bottling and then shipment of the wine. A steady, even flow − from the grapes arriving intact at one side of the cellar to the final product leaving from the other − helps to ensure that the goodness extracted from the vineyard is carried through into the bottle.

The second rule involves making maximum use of gravity when liquid is being transferred from stage to stage. It is believed that wine loses flavour when it is pumped, and although virtually all wine is moved by mechanical means at some time or another in the course of its making, cellar-masters prefer to keep such treatment to a minimum and rather allow the wine to move by means of gravitational flow. The Cape's geography, which allows cellars to be built on and into sloping ground, provides the ideal platform for this principle. Examples of its use can be clearly seen in cellars such as Morgenhof and Vergelegen, where the barrel storage cellar is below the fermentation tank level.

The actual process of making wine can be said to begin with the crushing of the grapes. This can be done to varying degrees: at one extreme the grapes are tumbled helter-skelter into the crusher and macerated, then compressed to extract the maximum amount of juice. Sometimes whole bunches of unbroken grapes are squeezed more gently and the most delicately flavoured juice is kept separate from liquid with a more robust character which is derived from near the skin tissue of the berry. At other times again, the juice of uncrushed and unpressed grapes is fermented by yeast cells that penetrate the skin. This procedure, which takes place in an enclosed tank and is known as anaerobic fermentation, is commonly used to make Beaujolais wines in France. In the Cape it is practised in cellars in the Paarl district during February and March, to make young wines for the annual Paarl Nouveau Festival.

The rich, succulent flavours of premium wines are fragile, requiring protection from summer heat and the potential ravages of oxygen. All South African cellars contain cooling

5

4. This is the entire maturation room of Camberley, one of the Cape's smallest cellars. 5. One of the larger ones, Vergelegen, is designed as a vertically orientated cellar, making use of the land's gradient.

equipment and closed tanks which allow wines to be fermented at any rate of conversion and at any temperature. The lower the temperature, the slower the rate of fermentation.

White wines are produced from only the juice of the grape, although the skins of white grapes, lacking any obvious colour, are sometimes steeped in the juice to add flavour. Generally, though, grape husks play little or no role in making white wines. Yeast added to the juice converts the grape's natural sugar into alcohol and carbon dioxide during the fermentation process. The wine is usually bottled soon after it emerges from the fermentation tank, or it may be allowed to mature in wood for a short time. As the accounts in the following pages will show, each wine-maker uses his experience and imagination to make the most of the resources at his disposal and produce an original series of masterpieces.

Rosé wines are made in the same way as white wines. The classic rosé type, *blanc de noir*, is made from the clear juice of red grapes which is lightly stained by the colour in the broken skins before the juice is drained off. Alternatively, rosé wines may be made simply by blending white and red wines.

2

Sparkling wines are created by incorporating carbon dioxide into a still wine, and this may be achieved through a number of different techniques. In the Cape one of the more popular means used is the making of bottle-fermented *cap classique*, following the *méthode champenoise* which derives from the Champagne region of France. In this method, a mixture of fermented wine, sugar and yeast is bottled and sealed. The yeast ferments the sugar in the blend, creating carbon dioxide which dissolves in the wine and adds a little more alcohol at the same time. At this stage the bottle contains a full-bodied wine, carbon dioxide at about six atmospheres of pressure, and a layer of dormant yeast deposited on the lower surface of the bottle.

A legal obligation for *cap classique* producers is to remove the yeast without losing anything of value from the wine. This is achieved by using gravity to shake the yeast down the side of the bottle into the neck, where it forms a small, flat cake on the cap. When the bottle is opened, the gas pressure blows the cake out, leaving the dissolved contents intact, and with a retained pressure of about four atmospheres. A small volume of wine with sugar dissolved in it is normally added to replace the liquid lost when the yeast was removed, and to balance the flavour with its comparatively high acid content.

3

Colour and an additional dimension of flavour is given to red wines by the inclusion of red grape skins when the juice is fermenting. In order to extract the maximum desired colour and flavour components from the skins, red wine-making involves special equipment and treatment during and after fermentation. Whereas fermenting white wine is a thin liquid, red wine in its formative stage contains a bulky mass of red grape skins. It has to be fermented in a wide-mouthed container that will allow the mountain of skins to be removed after the liquid wine has been drained off.

Fine red wines are normally matured in oak barrels. Between the alcohol-producing stage of fermentation and the long resting period known as maturation, most red wines go through a second fermentation, during which some of the minute volume of malic acid they contain is converted into lactic acid. This malolactic fermentation modifies the wine's flavour, adding softness and roundness, and normally occurs in tanks before the wine is transferred into barrels. Some wine-makers, however, prefer to move the wine into barrels directly after first-stage fermentation, and the malolactic fermentation takes place in the barrels. A red wine may remain in oak for between six months and two years before it is bottled.

4

1. Filling, racking (pumping out) and refilling barrels is one of the slowest jobs in the cellar. 2. Red grape skins are shovelled out of an open fermenter. 3. In an underground cellar cap classique *sparkling wine is steadily fermenting. 4. Skins left over from red wine fermentation have to be scraped out into the press by hand. 5. Dry grape skins form a ski-slope for the farm community's children.*

1

Vine by vine

'Making wine is a team thing,' says Jacques Borman of La Motte, in the Franschhoek valley. 'It's fantastic when you have responsible people to work with, like we have here. I can ask my team to come in on Easter Sunday night at 11 p.m. to help me, and then choose two from the group who offer. And that's on a farm where Easter is an important event. If you have that kind of work relationship, everything's a pleasure.'

2

There are more than 100 hectares of vineyard at La Motte, and the farm incorporates a small village of about 50 families. The men and women of the community are mostly employed in the estate's vineyards and cellar, and many have lived and worked in the same place for more than 15 years. The next stage in the plans for the community is the establishment of a retirement home on the farm.

'The most important asset we have is the right workforce,' says Jacques. 'And this comes from a long-term plan. You can't train a person to trellis vines in a year. Or how to work with canopy management. For this we need an ongoing programme. We send our staff on a lot of training courses where they learn things like how to do a better job when spraying, or trellising techniques for different varieties. They bring back many new ideas which benefit everybody here.'

Pietie le Roux is the vineyard manager at La Motte and directs the full viticultural programme. 'What we're aiming at is that the place can run itself,' explains Pietie. 'Recently we found ourselves in a situation where both Jacques and I had to be away

3

1. At La Motte, every row of vines is individually monitored, all year long. The growing conditions vary from mountain slope to river bank. 2. Pietie le Roux has a highly trained and motivated team of vineyard workers. 3. The barrel cellar, adjacent to the tasting room, is temperature- and humidity-controlled.

from the estate for a couple of weeks and the team here were running the whole farm on their own. When you can do that, when they run the farm better than you could have done, that's great.'

La Motte is an example of people harnessing nature and directing it towards an objective. With three widely varying soil types within its boundaries, this farm is comparatively difficult to cultivate and requires understanding, planning and careful treatment by informed people, in this case, the entire workforce. It encompasses roughly equal areas of granitic, loamy soil with a high clay content, low-fertility sandy soil with a clay underlayer, and fertile riverbank alluvials. To provide the estate cellar with a consistent supply of premium quality grapes from all parts of the farm, Pietie's staff implement a comprehensive, differentiated programme for each block, and in many cases the treatment varies from one row of vines to the next.

The objective of this painstaking programme is to produce balanced, richly flavoured wines. Without speedy harvesting at the ideal point of ripeness, block by block, much of the value of the year's work would be lost. Even after the grapes have been picked and the wine is being made, Jacques involves his team in evaluating the product during maturation to help co-ordinate their understanding and effort. 'We bring everyone working on the farm into the winery about two weeks after the last load of grapes has been offloaded and we start the tasting with the Sauvignon Blancs. Each tank of this sensitive variety is identified as to the block of vines it came from. Our workers can then taste the differences between blocks treated in different ways. And we repeat this process with every variety. Later in the year, we go through the whole thing again to see how each wine has developed.'

Each year the La Motte team experiments with yeast strains and fermentation techniques to vary flavours according to an individual vineyard's special characteristics. Thus vineyard and cellar workers are united in their efforts to constantly improve their product.

4

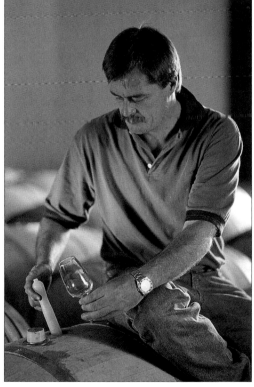

5

4. Wines made from individual vineyard blocks are kept apart, even in the cellar. 5. Jacques Borman, the cellar-master at La Motte, encourages all farm workers to evaluate the cellar's young wines.

1

Different personalities

'We have to treat all of our white grape varieties very differently to end up with the flavours we want in the bottle', says Ross Gower of Klein Constantia Estate. 'In the wine-making process, Sauvignon Blanc doesn't really add to the flavours you find in the vineyard at picking time. On the other hand, all the richness and fruit flavours of Chardonnay tend to develop with stimulation and time in the treatment you give it in the cellar.

'While you have to be ultra careful with Sauvignon Blanc and keep it away from air and oxygen, Chardonnay thrives on open-handed treatment. We give our Sauvignon Blanc grapes a dose of sulphur at the crusher as the first stage of protection against the potentially harmful effects of oxygen. Chardonnay first meets up with sulphur only when it comes out of the barrels, after it's been in the cellar for about eight months and has benefited a lot from controlled contact with oxygen.'

A third white variety made at Klein Constantia needs different treatment again. 'By contrast, Riesling has its own original programme.' Ross explains, 'All of our white grapes develop high acidity in the vineyard. While we lose some of the natural acidity in Sauvignon Blanc and Chardonnay in a deliberate programme of skin contact after crushing, we can't do that with Riesling. Our Riesling comes into the cellar with high acidity and a percentage of noble rot. We crush the grapes

2

4

1. For greater complexity in its wines, Klein Constantia vineyards are planted over a 300-metre variance in altitude. 2. The different white wines made at Klein Constantia require different treatment in the cellar. 3. Ross Gower measures the sugar content of grape juice.

and separate the juice from the skins as fast as possible so that we don't pick up any unwanted flavours. And I have to have a short fermentation, removing the yeast while there's still some sugar present, to make sure we have a balanced wine.'

Ross ferments the Sauvignon Blanc carefully at a slow, controlled rate and at a low temperature in stainless steel tanks. Meanwhile, in another part of the cellar, the fermentation of Chardonnay is started in a tank at a warm temperature and the liquid is then chilled to make the yeast inactive. The new must is pumped into 500-litre barrels where it warms up rapidly and the fermentation process continues at a temperature of about 20 °C until there is no sugar left. 'We then top up the barrels and wait for malolactic fermentation to begin of its own accord', continues Ross. 'When that is finished we gently stir the wine to remove carbon dioxide, and make sure that all the barrels are full before sealing them for a couple of months of maturation. During this period we stir up the lees that is at the bottom of each barrel every two weeks and let the wine develop naturally. In all of this time, no sulphur has been added.'

While the Chardonnay is looking after itself, the two more sensitive varieties are kept cold and comparatively sterile as they are shepherded along the process to the bottling line. The Riesling is painstakingly filtered and bottled, retaining the rich flavours and some of the grape sugar from the vineyard. The Sauvignon Blanc is left for about six weeks on some of the original fermentation lees at a low temperature, before being given the protection of bottle and cork at about mid-year.

Ross bottles the Chardonnay when its character has had sufficient opportunity to develop through contact with broken skins, yeast, oak barrels and air, and the malolactic fermentation process has given it a secondary dimension of flavours. This final step is taken between October and January.

5

4. Visitors are welcome to sample the estate's wines in its tasting and sales room. 5. Klein Constantia, a subdivision of the original Constantia estate, has one of the great Cape Dutch mansion homes.

1

2

3

Capturing fickle flavour

'Sauvignon Blanc goes through a lot of ups and downs. One day it's beautiful, the next it's heart-breaking. It's very temperamental. Shows one morning and by the next day it's hidden. But the longer you leave it, the smaller the differences become,' says Hermann Kirschbaum, cellar-master at Buitenverwachting in Constantia.

'About nine months after making, the wine seems to settle, and you finally know what you've got. All the up and down peaks and valleys are sort of mellowed. And after a year and a half to two years of waiting, if the wine is nice and rich, it's beautiful. I really like Sauvignon Blanc.' Hermann's annual love affair with Sauvignon Blanc starts all over again every February, with the assessing of the vineyards and their grapes' ripeness.

'With Sauvignon Blanc there are two styles,' says Hermann. 'There's the more grassy style and there's the more tropical, fat, sweeter fruit style. If you want a rich wine, you've got to choose the right vineyard and bring the grapes in really ripe. If you go for the grassy style – and because we have dramatic leaf and shoot growth in Constantia, we find it easy to make this type of Sauvignon – you have to pick it early. Once you have identified the style of wine the vineyard is suited to, you know whether you should pick early or late.'

Hermann makes his eventual decisions after eating thousands of grapes. 'Our vineyard manager and I walk through every vineyard block more and more often as the sugar content increases. In the end, we're in there every two days and we eat grapes and talk possible picking dates till our belts won't fit around our waists.' They pay a lot of attention to the weather. 'If we see rain coming and the grapes are ready and tomorrow is Saturday, we will pick all weekend. If you don't, what you were expecting to become a first-grade wine could become a fourth-grader.'

'We crush most of our Sauvignon Blanc grapes and allow the skins and juice to soak together, cold in a tank, for at least 12 hours. But sometimes, when you look at the grapes as they arrive at the cellar, you could just squeeze them and drink the juice straight. If I find

4

---

1. The gallery around the Buitenverwachting pressing cellar assists both the cellar-master and visitors to follow the activity. 2. The mountains behind the farm are just a few kilometres from both the Atlantic and Indian oceans. 3. Hosing down lug-boxes is one of the last of the daily tasks during the harvesting season.

that we have that kind of lovely flavour in the juice, and less in the skins, we squeeze the whole bunch, uncrushed, in the press and that delicious juice doesn't spend any time soaking with the skins.'

Hermann uses one of three different yeast strains for his Sauvignon Blanc. 'The one I choose depends on the speed of fermentation I want for that tank of wine', he says. 'I prefer to ferment at about 15 °C, which is fairly slow and careful, for about three weeks. While most Sauvignon Blanc wines are made to be drunk very fresh, I want to draw the maximum flavour from the yeast as well as the grape.' Hermann leaves each tank of wine with a fine bed of settled yeast for nine months before clarification. 'I'm sorry that all the Sauvignon Blanc shows and awards are over before I bottle my Sauvignon Blanc. I would also like to win some prizes. But the long yeast contact is part of this farm's style, so we will continue to wait until Christmas to bring out our Sauvignon Blanc.'

4. A pumpkin competition helps to enhance community spirit on the farm. 5. Buitenverwachting's double-storey cellar complex.
6. Hermann Kirschbaum and dogs, en route to testing his Sauvignon Blanc grapes for ripeness.

Working in miniature

'If you have great character in your grapes, you can manage to save that in your wine.' This sentiment, spoken by Mike Dobrovic of Mulderbosch Vineyards, is a common philosophy among wine-makers and can be seen in the practices followed at Mulderbosch, which lies north of Stellenbosch. The two key white wines made in the Mulderbosch cellar are Chardonnay and Sauvignon Blanc, each following a different path, with many deviations between vineyard and bottle. Mulderbosch is a small winery by South African standards, with less than 20 hectares of its own vineyards, in which both red and white varieties grow. This enables Mike to know each vineyard intimately. 'You can quite easily go through all of the vines, from bud break to harvest, and pick up a feel for what is happening in the season,' he says. 'That determines how I treat every vineyard, when we pick each one, how I work with the grapes and what I try to do with them, and what I try to do with the fermentation of each tank. We treat every block differently and we are trying to get the utmost out of each one.'

Every block has a selected picking point. 'You can determine your quality point right there,' says Mike. Sauvignon Blanc has 'hit-you-between-the-eyes' fruit flavour in both skins and juice that tells the wine-maker when to pick. These flavours develop to a point and then recede with the unstoppable process of ripening. Whereas Sauvignon Blanc is intolerant

1

2

1. Ripe grapes with differing sugar levels can be harvested from Mulderbosch vineyards on mountain slopes. 2. By Cape standards, Mulderbosch is a tiny property, currently encompassing just 16 hectares of vineyard. 3. Every Mulderbosch wine contains a percentage that has spent time in oak.

3

4

and punishes tardiness, Chardonnay is comparatively forgiving. 'The exquisite asparagus and green pepper flavours you could taste in the Sauvignon Blanc grapes may have disappeared forever if you delay picking for two days. With Chardonnay, though, richness may only have changed to succulence after a similar delay.'

Grape skins have to be broken and squeezed in a press to release all their liquid content. 'I only want the lovely, soft flavours that I can taste in the skins, so our pressing method, for both varieties, is no harder than the way the old people did it with their feet,' says Mike. Yeast converts the sugar in the grape juice to alcohol and carbon dioxide at between 12 °C and 30 °C. At the cooler temperature the process can take two to three weeks, while at 30 °C it's all over in a couple of days. Again, Sauvignon Blanc is the sensitive one, and Mike keeps his fermenting must away from oxygen and at a constant temperature.

A small volume of juice made from grapes allowed to ripen longer is fermented at warm temperatures in oak barrels to provide a contrasting flavour in the final blend. Chardonnay is more robust and even benefits from judicious oxygen contact and warm temperatures.

Although Chardonnay grape skins and juice are comparatively neutral in flavour in the vineyard, the familiar rich taste spectrum of this variety is enhanced by exposure to influences that Sauvignon Blanc would find damaging. Mike explains, 'I ferment Chardonnay in tanks and also in barrels. The tank fermentation of rich, sugary juice is allowed to race at 28 °C to give me a fat, creamy, buttery style, while more crisp juice is kept cooler, fermenting longer, making a fresher, more fragrant wine. The Chardonnay juice that is reserved for the barrels ferments at up to 25 °C and has controlled contact with oxygen.'

Mike allows both varieties to gain flavour from prolonged contact with the yeast, regardless of the original sweetness of the juice. Even tank-fermented Sauvignon Blanc spends months of maturation time with the yeast used in fermentation before being clarified. All the Chardonnay remains with the yeast for six to eight months before it is stabilised and bottled.

5

4. Grain crops grown between the rows of vines in winter and then dug in, contribute to the soil's composition. 5. Fynbos plants and their accompanying birds are encouraged on parts of the farm not dedicated to vineyards.

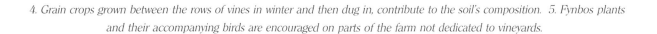

1

Au naturel

'The less you do to a wine, the better for the wine,' says Walter Finlayson, one of South Africa's foremost producers of premium Chardonnay. His policy of non-interference with nature has proved to be commercially successful at his Glen Carlou vineyard and cellar, outside Paarl. A series of full-bodied, barrel-fermented Chardonnays have resulted in many international awards, and has prompted investment in the cellar by Swiss businessman Donald Hess of the Hess Collection Winery in California.

2

1. The tasting room at Glen Carlou overlooks part of the fermentation cellar. Space for tanks is minimal, as most of the wine is barrel-fermented.
2. Glen Carlou welcomes visitors to taste its wines and a cheese that is produced on the farm.

3

4

5

Glen Carlou ranks as one of South Africa's leading barrel-fermented Chardonnay cellars, and this style of wine now accounts for more than two-thirds of the cellar's production. Walter's laid-back style created champion red wines from the vineyards of Blaauwklippen near Stellenbosch at an earlier stage in his career, but now he demonstrates his versatility by harnessing remarkable white wine flavours from Chardonnay vineyards planted on the warmer Paarl slopes.

When Walter and Jill Finlayson bought the Glen Carlou fruit farm in 1984, it had neither a cellar nor a Chardonnay vineyard. In 1988, when the first vineyard produced a small, unexpected crop, Walter found a spare pair of insulated railway containers, rolling stock and all, and used them to create a controlled-temperature home for all the barrels required for Chardonnay that year. The same containers have been used to make a substantial contribution to Glen Carlou's growing Chardonnay reputation every year since then. Each one holds 40 barrels and as they are separate units, the two batches can be fermented at different temperatures.

The Finlaysons' Chardonnay vineyards bear a comparatively small crop of five to six tons of grapes per hectare. They are harvested by hand when fully ripe, starting when the first vines reach 22.5° Balling and continuing helter-skelter until all the grapes are in the cellar, by which time the final loads are considerably riper. All the grapes are placed in 20-kilogram lug-boxes and the bunches are transferred directly into a press for gentle squeezing, without any additives. The resultant grape juice is cooled overnight to allow excess solid matter to settle and be removed, and the liquid is then pumped into barrels. Each barrel is inoculated individually with a yeast culture.

The insulated railway containers and Glen Carlou's new barrel fermentation cellar provide for temperature control of the environment, but Walter and his son David choose to ferment most barrels at the natural indoor temperature of 23 °C. A few barrels are encouraged to ferment at a warmer temperature, and others cooler so that they may contribute contrasting flavours for blending.

'Once the rapid fermentation has slowed down sufficiently, we fill all the barrels roughly to the maximum, and wait for the fermentation to finish and the malolactic fermentation to follow,' says Walter. 'We don't want all the barrels to have malolactic. We choose those with the fresh, fruity flavours and keep those cool. We allow approximately half our barrels to develop this secondary fermentation on their own.' Walter believes in natural development in the barrel. 'We leave the wines on the original fermentation lees in the barrel all winter. We taste regularly and we develop an evaluation record which is the basis of our blending plan, for when the wines are ready for bottling.'

The original fermentation yeast remains in the barrels for six to nine months, depending on the urgency of the bottling date and the rate of development of the wine. The yeast lying at the bottom of one-third of the barrels is stirred once a month. The other barrels are left with wine and yeast undisturbed.

The barrels themselves are an important ingredient in the wine-making process. 'We like to use a high proportion of new oak for our Chardonnays,' Walter explains. 'And I believe in using specialist coopers. I source my Chardonnay barrels from Burgundy coopers.'

Walter and David continue evaluating the wine throughout the fermentation process until they are ready to begin blending. 'We start tasting in May and try to delay bottling until as late in the year as possible.' The wines are blended and given a pre-filtration to remove solids, then are made stable in the cellar's chilling tanks before being bottled and labelled ready for sale.

3. Crushed white grapes are pumped to the press. 4. David (left) and Walter Finlayson check the rate of fermentation. 5. A gravel floor in the barrel room assists in humidity control.

1

Letting things happen

'When we are doing spontaneous fermentation with Chardonnay,' says Martin Meinert, cellar-master at Vergelegen, in Somerset West, 'all we do is put the juice in the barrel and leave it there. It takes about three or four days before it starts and it just runs along by itself. Sometimes fermentation takes a month, sometimes three or four months.' By letting nature take its course in this way, Martin has returned to the original process of wine-making, whereby the native yeast, found on the grape skins and in the air in the cellar, converts the grape juice to wine. 'We do nearly everything with Chardonnay in two different ways to give some extra choices and add complexity,' says Martin. 'We grow most of our Chardonnay high on the mountainside to get the greatest concentration, but we also grow some down in the valley, where it's warmer in summer but colder in winter. The high vineyards ripen a month after those below and are usually not ready to pick until after we have started with Cabernet Sauvignon, planted much lower.'

Some of the Chardonnay grape bunches are crushed to obtain the juice and some are simply squeezed in the press. 'We used to do only whole-bunch pressing, but I've introduced crushing to give a second set of crisper flavours. And we used to settle the solids in the juice to have a virtually clear liquid to ferment, but now we also work with cloudy, turbid Chardonnay juice. Spontaneous fermentation requires lots of solids in the juice to help the native yeasts get going.'

2

3

4

1. Vergelegen's modern cellar has an observation deck that covers three levels of activity, all below ground. 2. The Cape Dutch farmhouse at Vergelegen adjoins a garden complex, a restaurant and a visitors' centre, all of which are dominated by 300-year-old camphor trees.

Martin also works with cultured strains of yeast. 'We add this yeast culture to the selected juice in the tank and as soon as we see that the fermentation has started, we move the lot into barrels. I want a really warm fermentation, so we switch off the air-conditioning in the white wine barrel cellar and we let it ferment naturally at about 24 °C. While the spontaneous fermentation is working away slowly, the cultivated yeasts in the other barrels are in much higher concentrations and those fermentations are complete within two weeks. We're increasing our focus on the natural fermentation. It seems to give more of the kind of richly flavoured wine we want for our reserve Chardonnay.

'I like to have the effect of malolactic fermentation in Chardonnay, but some wines with gentle fruit flavours are preferable without. So we don't add the malolactic culture to those barrels. After malolactic and topping we stir all barrels at least once a week.'

The wines stay in wood through the winter and spring months. Bottling takes place in November and reserve Chardonnay from Vergelegen is released after a further six months of maturation in the bottle.

5

3. The main fermentation centre is flanked by the barrel-fermentation room for white wines. 4. All the vineyards at Vergelegen have been recently planted and cover a wide variation in altitude. 5. Martin Meinert, cellar-master at Vergelegen.

83

The dilemma of blending

'The three most important areas in trying to make great sparkling wine are choice of variety, pressing and blending. And the most important of them by far is blending.'

This is how Jeff Grier of Villiera Estate sees the major issues in his chosen speciality, bottle-fermented sparkling wine. 'Blending is a decision-making process that allows no turning back. If you get it right, you've got something you like. But if you make a mistake, you can't change a thing. And remember, when you're blending base wines for sparkling wine, you're dealing with complex issues that don't apply to the blending of dry white or red still wines. We blend low-alcohol still wines and have to make our choices knowing that this component will have to be re-fermented in the bottle, gain alcohol and millions of bubbles, attain an extra dimension of body and flavour, and further develop over five years or so before anyone tastes the product. That's why blending is the key point of all we do.'

Jeff has been making bottle-fermented sparkling wine by the *cap classique* method since 1984, when Jean-Louis Denois of Cumières in the Champagne region of France spent the harvest in the Villiera cellar, near Paarl. For several years after that, Jean-Louis came to Villiera for the Cape harvest at the beginning of the year and Jeff went to Champagne for the equivalent period later on, before the northern autumn. They also visited California and Australia together to see how and why grapes ripen differently in different conditions.

Champagne is made from technically under-ripe grapes. The base wine is re-fermented in bottles with additional sugar and yeast, producing a full-bodied wine with a higher alcohol content and a natural sparkle from trapped carbon dioxide. In Champagne this process is known as *méthode champenoise*, and in the Cape it is called *cap classique*. In the making of his sparkling wine, which is sold under the Tradition label, Jeff's team has to make low-alcohol base wines from grapes that are less than fully ripe. But as grapes develop more quickly at the Cape than they do in Champagne, the strict champagne recipe doesn't work neatly. 'We have to find our own ideal harvesting point for each variety,' Jeff says. 'But with experience, you get a feeling. We taste our grapes many times a week, pre-harvest, and I believe you can almost taste the sparkling wine in the grapes. When it tastes right, we pick. There are four varieties we work with. We have Chardonnay and Pinot Noir, the classic champagne varieties, and we have Chenin Blanc and Pinotage, the varieties we found on the farm when we arrived here. From these we make about 15 different styles of base wine, barrel-fermented, tank-fermented, barrel-matured, malolactic, and so on. And these different wines have to be blended together in the right proportion for each of our four products.'

The secondary fermentation process known as malolactic fermentation happens naturally and is a standard feature of champagne. Few Cape producers of *cap classique* allow it to happen to their bubbly base wines as it diminishes total acidity, a comparatively fragile component in most South African wines. Many of Villiera's base wines, however, are characterised by high acidity and consequently Jeff welcomes malolactic fermentation in about half of those that go into the Tradition blend.

In the making of deluxe products, the policy for the Tradition wines is that they undergo maturation on the yeast in the bottle for up to four years, and maturation on the cork for a further 12 months before they are added to the sales list. An exception is Tradition's Carte Rouge, which first makes a market appearance after 18 months of maturation in the bottle, and two or three months of cork maturation.

1

2

4

3

1. Making sparkling wines by the cap classique *method requires riddling the yeast into the neck of the bottle. At Villiera this is done both by hand and mechanically.*

2. Cap classique *bottles are ready for labelling after they have been disgorged, dosed and corked. 3. When fermentation in the bottle is complete, the yeast is removed.*

5

6

4. To make sparkling wine, uncrushed grapes are squeezed in a press, producing free-run juice. 5. Jeff Grier evaluates the progress of barrel-fermented base wine.
6. Villiera's mechanised riddlers replicate the movements made by hand during the traditional process of shaking down the yeast.

Maintaining control under pressure

'I believe you have to talk to your barrels individually,' says Pieter Ferreira, cellar-master in the Graham Beck sparkling wine cellar. 'And so I add the yeast solution to every individual barrel.' The Graham Beck Madeba cellars, near Robertson, are characterised by carefully worked-out practices, with every stage of the sparkling wine production planned and monitored. Thus, yeast is added to Chardonnay juice in each barrel, instead of to the juice in the tank before it is transferred into barrels, as is standard practice. Pieter explains, 'We want to gain the most out of this one oxidative stage in sparkling wine production, so we make sure all the fermentation happens in the barrel. We don't want it to start in the tank.'

Madeba's Chardonnay vineyards are all planted in limestone-rich soils, while the Pinot Noir vines have been allocated to alluvial soil with a riverstone base. The Chardonnay for barrel fermentation has been planted in rows that run north to south, designed to provide grapes with the highest acidity levels. 'We used to worry about the noticeable fruit flavours in our Chardonnay grapes when the sugar was still comparatively low. Now we know that this is one of the main things that make our sparkling wines different.'

All the grapes are picked in 20-kilogram lug-boxes, and all the juice is obtained by pressing whole bunches. Following the traditional champagne practice of separating the free-run first juice from the pressed-out second juice, the Madeba cellar ferments these fractions separately. The decision to use any wine made from pressed juice is left to the final evaluation of blend components, before bottling.

Madeba commissions a batch of tiny champagne piece barrels for every vintage. 'We use our champagne piece barrels to ferment selected Chardonnay juice and give it a warm, open, soft flavour to add complexity to our top blends,' says Pieter. This is a warm fermentation, with the sugar conversion process running quickly at about 24 °C. 'The wine only stays in the oak for eight weeks. This is long enough to convert all the sugar and settle most of the solids to provide us with clear young wine.'

The barrels are emptied and the wine is prepared for evaluation along with about 20 other Chardonnay and Pinot Noir base wines, before the final blends are decided. The blends have

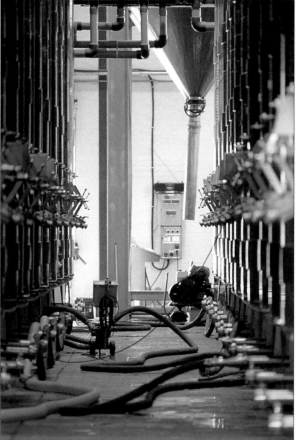

2

1

3

1. The Graham Beck vineyards share the hot and dry Robertson valley with typical Karoo vegetation. They produce a fruity flavour in the grape, at low ripeness levels. 2. Pieter Ferreira must decide the best point at which to remove the base wine from the barrels.

4

5

to be finalised before the important stage of second fermentation in the bottle can begin. The barrel-fermented and tank-fermented wines are brought to the assessment table in March and blend decisions are made before April ends.

When the individual Chardonnay and Pinot Noir wines have been selected for each of the farm's products and blends are ready for combination, a concentrated culture of yeast cells is developed in a base wine solution. This is added to a sugar and wine combination which, in turn, is added to the blend. The newly active, fermenting liquid is poured into the familiar pressure-resistant bottle, where it will stay until it is drunk. The bottles are kept at about 12 °C in a climatically controlled room until the development of the bubble and the yeast-enhanced flavours is considered complete. At Madeba the non-vintage blend of Pinot Noir and Chardonnay is given 24 months of yeast contact in the secondary stage in the bottle, while the cellar's vintage product is given 48 months of ageing. After this extended waiting period, the bottles are riddled mechanically to shake the yeast down into the neck before it is removed by disgorging, sugar is added and the bottles are corked.

3. The Graham Beck cellar has been furnished with ultra-modern equipment. 4. The tasting room looks out on vineyards, with dry Karoo hills beyond.
5. Pupitres enable the yeast inside the bottle to be slowly shaken down into the cap before being removed.

1

Finding the balance

'Everything to do with quality is connected with the balance of the vine,' says Gyles Webb of Thelema Mountain Vineyards, just outside Stellenbosch. 'I want to improve the quality of the fruit while increasing the quantity of the crop. I don't believe that the smaller the crop, the better the wine. You need to get your vine growing in balance with your conditions – the soil fertility, the moisture and temperature, and so on – and then you need a serious crop of grapes that the plant is able to ripen fully. There's no such thing as a standard-sized crop. Every vineyard is different, and as a wine-maker you're better off spending your time working out what you can do about it than sticking around in the cellar.

'The worst Merlot I ever made was from a tiny crop. I make much richer and more rewarding Merlots from larger crops. In many cases, when a plant is stressed by drought, for instance, a small crop works out very well, but when you're looking at healthy vines, the balance is the thing.'

Thelema's vineyards, sited on the southeast-facing slopes of the Simonsberg, are among the highest in the Stellenbosch area. The blocks of vines are planted at altitudes of between 370 and 550 metres above sea level in soils that are deep, formed from decomposed granite, and strikingly red in colour with a significant clay content. They are surprisingly fertile, providing much more vigorous plant growth than on most other Stellenbosch farms. 'That's where the difficulties start,' says Gyles. 'I can't learn too much from the other producers in the valley

2

3

1. Thelema's vineyards are the scene of constant experimentation in an endeavour to combine quality and quantity. 2. Gyles Webb, the driving force at Thelema. 3. More than 1200 barrels are used to mature the produce of 35 hectares.

4

5

because their problems are different. There weren't any vineyards at Thelema before we bought the place, so we have had to learn everything from scratch.

'You know, wine-making is really a piece of cake,' he maintains. 'There are books about wine-making, but nothing on viticulture that can tell me how to look after any block of vines on this place. Sauvignon Blanc is a perfect example. It's a variety that can't handle stress during ripening. The moment there's pressure on the crop, the flavour disappears. And yet, with our fertile soil and dramatic growth potential, we need to hold back the plant between flowering and berry set so that we don't get an excess of green growth. Then when the crop is developing and ripening, we have to release the brakes and have as little stress as possible. We treat every row differently. In one, for example, we've removed every second vine to give each plant twice as much space.

'In our farm plan, every Sauvignon Blanc block has an ideal balance of plant material to crop size. We monitor the green growth constantly. You'll find us charging around the vines with our pruning shears, ready to rip off any excess shoots. Once you have the crop in balance and developing healthily, the worst thing you can do is to pick at the wrong time. If we picked Sauvignon Blanc at 21° Balling we'd have lots of acid, no flavour, terrible wine. So we are forced to find ripeness at high sugar levels. I do every kind of analysis of juice, I taste the grapes and I look at the vines a lot. The moment I see some vines looking tired, we take the crop off.'

Thelema is run by a very small team, with Gyles taking the creative lead all the way from soil preparation to barrel fermentation. His hands-on technique puts him in the forefront of South Africa's quest to make a mark as a New World wine-producer.

4. Although Gyles is considered to be one of the leading wine-makers in the Cape, he spends more time in the vineyards than he does in the cellar. 5. Thelema's neatly designed modern cellar.

Forty times a day

Plunge, lift. Plunge, hoist. Push down, heave up. That's the rhythm of life at Kanonkop in February and March. All day and all night.

Looking across the cellar's chessboard of open, rectangular fermenting tanks, the scene is dominated by the continuous punching down of wooden-shafted paddles that are used to break up the coagulated mass of red grape skins floating on top of the fermenting must in each tank. Wielding the paddles are a dozen cellar-workers who stand on the sides of the tanks and punch down through the grape skins, mixing the fermenting liquid with the broken skins that instantly rise again to the top.

Each tank is subjected to a complete punching-down about 40 times every 24 hours, until more than two-thirds of the sugar content has been converted into alcohol. Then the rate drops to half a dozen times a day, and when fermentation has removed almost all the sugar, the skins and liquid are separated. The skins are squeezed in a mechanical press to obtain the last of the liquid, and the slowly fermenting must is pumped into a closed concrete tank so that the sugar-conversion process can be completed.

But this is not where it all begins. For Beyers Truter, the cellar-master at Kanonkop, wine-making starts in the vineyard. The first of the creative decisions made by the wine-maker for each vintage is choosing the moment when the grapes are fully ripe. Beyers has strong feelings about waiting for this moment. 'There's no such thing as a light-bodied red wine. You have to have balance in a special wine and all the elements have to be in harmony. Picking time is the most crucial period in the making of wine because once you've picked those grapes, that's all you've got to work with.' As harvest time approaches, 'I go into the vineyard a lot, and spend my life eating grapes. When I am sampling Pinotage, or any variety, I chew the berry and spit it out. If the colour is dark, then it's ripe and we pick.'

Not only does Beyers start off the fermentation process in open tanks that, in principle, have remained unchanged for a hundred years, but he also selects a high proportion of fruit from old vines for all Kanonkop's top wines. 'When a vine has reached 12 years, you've worked out the size of the leaf canopy needed and the quantity of grapes that each vine should carry. You invariably get excellent fruit from these vines.'

He removes the stems from the bunches before crushing and adds sulphur to the grapes to prevent spontaneous malolactic fermentation during the open-tank stage. 'I use a slow-fermenting yeast and try to keep the temperature of the fermenting must to around 30 °C. And then we punch night and day. You can only get the soft tannins and fruit flavours out of the skins during the first two or three days of fermentation, and I want the maximum mixing during this period.' Comparatively long and wide, the Kanonkop open fermenters create shallow pools of mash, giving maximum contact between juice and skin.

The mash of skins left in the tanks after the must has been removed is pressed hard, regardless of variety, and all this richly tannic must is added to the main volume. Pinotage is generally separated and pressed at an earlier and sweeter stage than the other red varieties, which stay two days longer in the open tanks. However, all the red varieties are moved into the closed tanks to complete the fermentation process separate from the skins.

KANONKOP

1

2

---

1. Virtually all Kanonkop wine is matured in the barrel. Beyers Truter keeps a record of every barrel's development. 2. Kanonkop's vineyards, running across the foreground, are on lower mountain slopes. 3. A sample of fermenting grape must is prepared for analysis of its sugar content. 4. When grown on a bush vine, Pinotage grapes have deeply coloured skins. 5. To obtain maximum colour and soft tannins, the cellar team punches the grape skins down through the cap.

3

4

'We use our concrete tanks to finish the fermentation because they have natural insulation and the must cools down only a couple of degrees during the transition. I want the fermentation to finish quickly, and maintaining a warm temperature helps,' says Beyers. 'I also try to have the malolactic process over as quickly as possible, and I induce it in my concrete tanks as soon as the alcoholic fermentation is over.'

All the estate's main red wines are matured in barrels. At present the complement comprises one-third each of new, second-fill and third-fill barrels. 'Pinotage loves new oak, and I get the best combination of soft tannins and fruit flavours from my new oak barrels.' The wines chosen for the new oak casks are transferred into them during April and May, when malolactic fermentation is complete. The older barrels are filled in June and July. At Kanonkop Pinotage spends less time in the barrel than other red varieties. Beyers finds that 'Pinotage has completed the flavour development process, and the fruit and oak components are fully integrated within the first 12 months in the cask. Cabernet and Merlot are kept in wood normally for between 18 months and two years.'

Like most wine-makers, he is wary of the effects of clarification of his wines. In removing sediment and solid matter, the over-zealous polishing of wines can take out hard-earned flavours. The wines matured in older barrels are in greater need of clarification than those in new oak, and he generally fines them with egg white after between six and nine months. Kanonkop's wines are bottled after blending and final filtration, generally without the addition of any extra acidity.

Although Beyers Truter's ways may be described as 'old style', he is setting benchmark standards in giving his red wines maximum soft tannins and fruit flavour.

5

Picking perfect grapes

'When I can see that virtually all the red grapes in one of the vineyards have changed colour, the stage we call "veraison", we go into that vineyard and remove any green grapes,' says Nico van der Merwe of Saxenburg. 'If you don't, you get some grapes that are unripe going into the crusher with your carefully tended, fully ripe grapes. We do this separation of levels of ripeness with all our red varieties. There's nothing more important than having only fully, evenly ripe grapes to crush and ferment. If you have a small crop of five or six tons per hectare of grapes like this, you can hardly fail to make marvellous wine.

'I try to have Merlot and Cabernet Sauvignon on cool slopes, and planted in fertile soil. I want fatness on the middle palate for Cabernet Sauvignon and intensity of fruit in the Merlot. But Shiraz is the odd one out. I want my Shiraz growing in less fertile soil, on a warmer site, and I want to see this variety struggle a bit.'

Nico adds, 'Shiraz is the only variety where I deliberately leave part of the crop to get to be almost over-ripe. The berries' skins will have started to shrivel. These grapes give juice with an extra dimension of flavour. In a cooler season, I look for even more of these wrinkly grapes.'

The picking time, Nico believes, is important. 'I prefer to pick all our red

1. Facing two oceans, Saxenburg's slopes provide a number of different growing and ripening conditions. 2. Helmeted guineafowl can be seen scratching for food all over the farm. The bird has become a key element in the farm's label design, and lends its name to the restaurant.

grapes in the afternoon if I can. I want these grapes to arrive at the cellar freshly picked and warm from the sun. We don't use sulphur at the crusher and I want to add yeast to the crushed juice and start fermentation as soon as possible. We ferment all our reds at between 30 °C and 32 °C, and that gives us the colour and flavour extraction that has created our style. We use the slow-fermenting South African cultured yeast and that gives us a wine with an alcohol content of around 13° after three or four days at those temperatures.'

'We ferment dry on the skins and use all the pressed wine in the main blend. The wine is still warm when it goes into our concrete storage tanks, and it soon starts malolactic fermentation. All our reds are in oak barrels before the end of May, and they stay there for a year. The wines have very little handling or treatment.'

Before being pumped into the barrels, the wines are chilled to about 12 °C so that the solids in them tend to settle. Then they are racked, which is a process of draining the liquid top part of the tank's contents off the thicker material that has settled to the bottom.

'We try to reduce the period that the wine spends between the barrel and the bottle to as little as possible,' says Nico. 'The wine has enhanced its colour and flavours in the barrel and these lovely characters must be protected by bottling as soon as possible. So we give the wines a light egg-white fining and filter before we bottle them. We generally keep our bottled wines for a resting period to settle down before we release them. These reds are generally made available between two and three years after the harvest.'

4

---

3. All Saxenburg's red wines are matured in the barrel in the farm's functional cellar. 4. Nico van der Merwe measures the sugar content of the juice before fermentation begins. The process will continue for several days.

1. In the circular barrel cellar at Morgenhof, the temperature and humidity are maintained at one level all year. 2. The ornamental garden above the cellar. From relative obscurity some years ago, the estate has been developed into one of the Cape's prime function venues.

3

Heat and light

'I'm trying to get behind the reason for the French success with red wines,' says Jean Daneel, the wine-maker at Morgenhof, just north of Stellenbosch. 'The best ones have very soft, velvety tannins, and this is created in the vineyards.'

'Our ripening cycle here at the Cape is very different from theirs. We are closer to the equator and have more intense light. Generally it is also much warmer here. And Cabernet Sauvignon and Merlot ripen in their own ways. In Bordeaux, when you kick against the stem of a full, ripe vine, almost half the berries fall to the ground. At that point, the juice in those grapes has enough sugar to make 13° of alcohol. If we wait for our grapes to reach this physical point of ripeness, we could only make port, the wine would be so high in alcohol. So we have to work hard to find the ideal point of ripeness for each variety.' Jean adds, 'When you can slide the grape skin easily off the flesh, that berry is pretty ripe. When the skin releases lots of red colour into the juice as you're chewing it, then you're ready to pick.'

The different varieties have their own requirements. 'We can create our best opportunities by finding the right piece of land for each variety and modifying the quantity of leaf growth and the size of the crop. Merlot needs the coolest spots on the farm to do best, and has a naturally bigger crop than Cabernet Sauvignon. We thin out some of the Merlot bunches early in the season, so we end up with a crop of about six tons per hectare of each variety.'

Both Cabernet Sauvignon and Merlot are fermented at between 25 °C and 30 °C in stainless steel tanks. 'We don't have heaters in our tanks, so if we have cool weather, we compensate by building up a high concentration of yeast in the fermenting must, and the increased yeast activity pushes up the temperature.' Jean pumps the liquid from the bottom of the tank to shower over the top of the skins which are floating on the surface. This mixing cycle ensures that all the juice has opportunity to gain colour and flavour from the skins.

The closed tanks allow Jean to leave the skins and wine together after fermentation with little risk of oxidation. This process, known as maceration, is designed to allow grape tannins, extracted from the skins, to soften in flavour. Once the liquid has been drained out of the fermentation tanks, the small percentage of wine remaining in and between the skins has to be squeezed out in the press. 'I don't want to extract too much tannin from my Merlot,' says Jean. 'There's a point where the hard flavours begin to dominate. I press Merlot slowly and taste the must often to find the point to stop. In this way, I get only the flavours I want in my wine. Cabernet Sauvignon is easier. I can use more of the pressed must in the final blend and it gives an added richness and mouth feel to the wine.'

All the Cabernet Sauvignon and Merlot wines are matured in small French oak casks in an underground cellar, where the temperature remains about 16 °C all year. The red wines are removed for clarification and bottling after they have spent 18 months to two years in oak.

4

---

3. Morgenhof's neatly cultivated vineyards are terraced up the steep slopes of the foothills of the Simonsberg.
4. Jean Daneel, cellar-master at Morgenhof, models his wines on the French style.

A new angle on a dog's life

Lovers of the new style of South African Shiraz, or Syrah as this trend-setting wine made at Stellenzicht is known, will be surprised to hear that it was all started by a dog. One Friday evening in the middle of the 1994 harvest Dikke, an overweight Labrador, was discovered surrounded by stripped stems of grape bunches and chewing on mouthfuls of the black berries. Distracted by the dog's enthusiasm, Dikke's owner, André van Rensburg, helped himself to some of the dog's grapes. The combination of vivid flavours and intense sweetness of those couple of grapes changed the course of André's Friday evening, the weekend leisure plans of his farm workers, and the general style of Shiraz wine-making.

André left his dinner to harden in the warming drawer as he arranged for the whole farm labour force to pick grapes the following day. For the first time in Stellenzicht's history, grapes were harvested and crushed throughout a Saturday.

1. At Stellenzicht, white wines are fermented in closed containers under chilled conditions. 2. The Syrah process, on the other hand, develops in open fermenters. 3. The crop of Syrah at Stellenzicht is small and concentrated.

'Those grapes were so luscious, so wonderful, I just had to have them immediately in the cellar,' says André. 'That is what fully ripe means to me. When you finally find grapes like that you have to do your best to keep all of that flavour in the wine. But my problem was, I didn't have a clue where Dikke had found those bunches. I didn't know if it was Cabernet Sauvignon, Merlot or Shiraz. I had only been on the farm for a couple of months and I had to check the varieties growing near to my house on a map of Stellenzicht's vineyards. It was dark when I went into the Shiraz vineyard next to my house, but I found the grapes there were just like the ones in the Labrador's paws. The skins were black, some were wrinkled. The grapes had rich fruit flavour and loads of sugar.

'We managed to pick almost all six hectares of Syrah, as we call this wine, that Saturday morning, which probably had a lot to do with the eventual quality. And now that we had a cellar full of very ripe grape juice, we used a very simple technique. The mash was fermented in open fermenters, with lots of pumping over. The temperature of the liquid was high, and all of the sugar was fermented out with the skins still in the mixture. After leaving it for a couple of days, I gave the skins a gentle pressing and put this new, rich, deep-coloured Syrah into small French oak barrels. That first year, I had very little new wood, but every drop of the wine went into barrels.'

In subsequent seasons André's method has changed very little. He now puts 30 per cent of each vintage of the young Syrah into new American oak each year. The wine continues to spend 12 months in small oak, a further six months in 5000-litre oak vats and then, after an egg-white fining, is bottled without filtration.

There is only one Syrah vineyard on Stellenzicht. It is planted on granitic Helderberg soil, heavy in clay content. The vines carry few bunches of grapes and produce little more than four tons per hectare. No changes to any part of the system are planned. The Syrah harvest starts only when Dikke decides that the grapes are ready to eat.

4. André van Rensburg at the loading bin. 5. Syrah grapes gain a high sugar content on the granite-based red soils of the lower slopes of the Helderberg. 6. A lug-box of Syrah grapes is emptied into the crusher.

Sleepless nights

'Somehow it's always in the middle of the night when a tank of port is ready for fortification, so that night you don't sleep,' says Anton Bredell of J.P. Bredell Wines. 'We do about 20 tanks of port during a harvest, and there's a lot of sleep lost in making sure that the fermentation in each one stops just where you want it to.'

The first stage of port-making is very similar to the traditional Cape technique used to make dry red wine, but the raging fermentation in the intensely tannic, sweet red must has to be stopped with the addition of distilled grape spirit at the point where the wine has its most balanced flavour.

'It's a very slow process,' explains Anton. 'To achieve harmony between the brandy spirit and the fruit and grape tannin, the alcohol has to be added bit by bit.' Using this technique, the yeast cells are still slowly fermenting sugar even after all the alcohol has been added to the tank. The rate of sugar conversion slows over the next couple of hours until it stops completely. If the brandy spirit is added rapidly, the yeast is shocked into inactivity and the resulting port wine is hard and slow to develop to maturity.

Anton Bredell makes port wine from the traditional port varieties, most of which were imported into South Africa by Professors Perold and Theron during the first half of the twentieth century. The first port varieties were planted on the J.P. Bredell farm during 1942, and port-style wines have been made there ever since. The farm, which lies on the eroded lower slopes of the Helderberg no more than about three kilometres from False Bay, has a mixture of sandy and Helderberg granite soils. The vines are grown without irrigation in order to produce small crops.

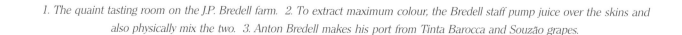

Anton's preferred Portuguese varieties, Tinta Barocca and Souzão, have been chosen for the intensity of the tannic content of their skins, rather than for fruit flavours. Their grapes are allowed to ripen until, in the case of Tinta Barocca, the skins begin to wrinkle and the sugar content is between 24° and 26° Balling. The grape juice is very sweet, retaining

1. The quaint tasting room on the J.P. Bredell farm. 2. To extract maximum colour, the Bredell staff pump juice over the skins and also physically mix the two. 3. Anton Bredell makes his port from Tinta Barocca and Souzão grapes.

5

6

plenty of acidity. Fermentation takes place in traditional open fermenters, with the grape skin cap being punched down into the fermenting must rapidly and regularly over the first two days to extract the maximum colour and tannin.

'The character of the vintage determines if I'm going to make vintage quality port and also which vineyard block will be used for this most special wine,' Anton tells us. 'Though half a dozen blocks may have the required sweetness at picking, I have to taste the grapes regularly to find the block with the richness of tannin and juice flavours that will give the flavour and structure we need for vintage quality. I also smell the fermenting must a lot. It's very difficult to taste quality at this early stage, but when I pick up a type of liquorice smell, I know I'm on the right track.'

As the level of sweetness drops to near the point needed for fortification, Anton separates the liquid must from the skins. Brandy spirit is added to lift the total alcohol level to 19 per cent and this causes the rate of fermentation to slow to a halt. The wine is then chilled in a tank to encourage the lees to settle before it is transferred into the used 500-litre barrels in which it will age. Vintage quality port remains untouched in these barrels for two years before being racked off the lees and then bottled without being either clarified or filtered.

4. The vineyards from which the port grapes come are located on the middle slopes of the Helderberg, near Somerset West. 5. The complex of cellar buildings dates from the 1940s. 6. Anton Bredell pumps Tinta Barocca must onto the skins to extract maximum colour and flavour.

2

3

1   4

Dessert wines and fortified wines

Most of the world's wines are sold with a certain degree of sweetness that is either retained in the juice during fermentation or added to it afterwards. This fractional amount of sugar is often masked by the natural acidity in the grapes. In a special category are wines with pronounced sweetness, and these range from handcrafted classics made from the fermented juice of over-mature, sugar-saturated fruit – some of which are fortified with additional alcohol – to unfermented grape juice which is preserved with alcohol. The latter is a curiosity which barely deserves to be called a wine as it has not undergone the fermentation process, but it is generally grouped with other fortified wine products.

In the making of dessert wines, the yeast modifying the sugar in the grape juice during the fermentation process is stopped in its tracks when the ambient temperature of the liquid drops below 10 °C or, in the case of fortified wines, when the alcohol in the liquid is boosted to more than 16 per cent of the total. When the yeast is removed, the wine that results has the flavour of what is left of the original grape juice.

In the Cape there are two important dessert wine styles that, made without fortification, contain alcohol derived only from the yeast fermentation of the grape juice. One of these is Special Late Harvest, which is made from very ripe grapes that have benefited from the dehydrating and flavour-enhancing fruit fungus called *Botrytis cinerea*. By regulation, it must contain between 30 and 50 grams of sugar per litre. The second, Noble Late Harvest, is produced from even riper grapes which have been shrunken by *Botrytis cinerea* and contain about a third sugar. Once again, all the alcohol is derived from the yeast fermentation.

Botrytis cinerea is a fungus which settles in the grape skin and allows moisture to evaporate without permitting any other organism or material to penetrate. The flavour in the grape juice is thus concentrated, and the grape gains sweetness without losing acidity. Whenever a grape grower notices the fungus in his vineyard, he will either instruct his harvesting team to pick quickly before the infection can spread or, if he intends to make a Special or Noble Late Harvest wine, he will leave the grapes and allow the outbreak to develop. A 48-hour period of high humidity when the grapes are at just the right level of ripeness provides ideal conditions for the fungus to spread rapidly, reducing a yield of ten tons to five or even three. Proximity of the vineyard to the sea is an advantage as it ensures the humidity required.

Only some of the grapes in a bunch are affected by the fungus, so the wine is made from a percentage of normally over-ripe grapes and some blackened, wizened ones. In the making of Noble Late Harvest, the bunches are harvested by hand and, at the cellar, they are squeezed slowly and gently. The juice is chilled to around 5 °C, staying at that temperature for several days so that as much solid matter as possible settles to the bottom of the tank.

Fermentation then begins, and as it occurs in the cooler weather at the end of summer it can take a long time, even months. Some wine-makers like to ferment part of the wine in barrels, achieving flavours that complement those gained in the tank. The yeast continues to convert sugar until it has produced the required balance of alcohol and sugar. The wine then stays in oak or tank for seven to 11 months before being clarified and bottled.

Sherries and ports are fortified with additional alcohol and made at the Cape much as they are elsewhere. Variations on the theme include South African specialities such as Hanepoot (made from Muscat d'Alexandrie grapes) and white and red muscadels.

5

6

1. Sherry is aged progressively in a solera system, with the oldest wines in the lowest level of barrels. 2. Botrytis cinerea allows moisture to escape from the grape but protects the flavour of the juice that will make Noble Late Harvest. 3. Flor yeast coats the surface of maturing sherry, allowing controlled oxidation. 4. Nederburg is South Africa's largest producer of Noble Late Harvest. 5, 6. Dessert wines made at Buitenverwachting and Klein Constantia respectively merit special bottles.

1

Pots and oak – making brandy

While supplying grapes for a thriving wine industry and fresh fruit for domestic and export markets, South African vineyards also provide the raw material for one of the world's largest brandy producers. Approximately half as much brandy is made in South Africa each year as is distilled in the Cognac region of France. Yet comparatively little of it is exported; South Africa is also one of the largest brandy markets, consuming almost all the Cape's output.

The practice of distilling part of the Cape wine crop is almost as old as wine-making itself in the former Dutch colony. In the days before science allowed wine to be preserved, it was an essential part of the annual cycle of wine-making to distil a concentrated spirit that could travel with impunity. As farmers and other settlers moved away from Cape Town in the seventeenth, eighteenth and nineteenth centuries, supplies of brandy moved with them, and the brandy trade from the Cape to the interior became a major business.

The brandy produced then was invariably made in a primitive way, by boiling wine and then clarifying the raw concentrate that was yielded. Undoubtedly the flavour and quality

2

1. Cape brandy must, by law, contain at least 30 per cent pot-still brandy matured in oak. 2. The original pot still used by René Santhagen is preserved at the Oude Molen Brandy Museum. 3. Wine is distilled and then redistilled in pots such as these to produce brandy.

varied, but overall it seems that Cape brandy had an unsavoury reputation. Until the beginning of the twentieth century, the only laws relating to brandy involved the collection of taxes for the colonial authorities, and the governing of rowdy behaviour by consumers. Then, in 1897, the arrival of a certain René Santhagens in South Africa set in motion a chain of events that saw the use of pot stills, barrel maturation and minimum standards of distillation being incorporated into laws that form the basis of today's brandy industry.

A distiller trained in Cognac, Santhagens arrived at Stellenbosch in 1903. He began a largely single-handed campaign to improve the equipment and techniques used to make Cape brandy and to entrench these in general practice. He imported pot stills from Cognac and oak casks from Limousin and, while others were establishing the first wine co-operatives in 1905, he founded the first brandy co-operative in the same year.

Santhagen's pioneering techniques were incorporated into the first brandy production laws, passed in 1909 and 1924, enabling South Africa to benefit from stringently enforced standards of excellence and uniformity. Its brandy must contain no less than 30 per cent pot-still, oak-matured brandy, while the remainder can only be made from wine spirit. In this respect the Cape shares with Cognac the distinction of being the world's only brandy producers obliged to use pot-still distillation and small-barrel maturation in all products.

The pot-still technique involves a distilling kettle that heats wine and separates, collects and condenses the evaporating alcohol that results. When the alcohol is separated in a pot still, many other flavour components are concentrated and carried over into the condensed spirit, contributing to the brandy's richness of flavour. Compared with other forms of distilling apparatus, a pot still – which has remained unchanged in principle since distilling was invented – is more efficient in concentrating flavours than in separating alcohol. To make brandy, the liquid has to pass through the pot still twice: the first time yields a mild concentration of grape flavour and the second provides the richly flavoured spirit that goes into the oak and emerges eventually as Cape brandy. Other forms of distilling apparatus separate the alcohol more efficiently, but they lose most of the flavour along the way.

The KWV produces more than half of South Africa's brandy, operating five distilleries in different regions. Most is sold by the owners of major brands, liquor trading and marketing companies, some of which also operate commercial distilleries. Several wine co-operatives incorporate distilleries, producing brandy for the KWV and the brand owners. Changes to the distilling laws in 1990 have seen the re-introduction of estate or boutique brandy products, made entirely in pot stills in farm distilleries, following the practice in Cognac. These products can be sampled along with wines throughout the Cape winelands.

4. Some Cape estates are now also producing hand-crafted brandies. 5. The pot still used in the small farm distillery at Backsberg.
6. At the other end of the scale, the still room at KWV is one of the largest in the world.

1

2

3

4

5

Barrels and coopering

Long before glass bottles were invented, wine was stored and transported in wooden barrels, and coopering was an important industry throughout Europe. Even in those times there was a major commercial market in wines, and the grape growers of Spain, Italy, Portugal, Germany and France supplied wine to their domestic and export markets – the latter chiefly in western Europe – in small, manageable barrels. This was the practice from the fifteenth century until the twentieth, and even as recently as 60 years ago, more wine was shipped for export in barrels than in bottles.

Historically, many different woods were used to make wine barrels, but oak was reliable in many ways and became the preferred material, particularly in France. In time, after glass and ceramic bottles and then steel tanks were invented, the use of oak barrels for storage and for maturation declined, and by the second half of this century was comparatively limited. Wine lovers then discovered that in many cases they preferred the taste of wine that had spent a formative time in casks made from the oak tree.

There are many theories about what happens to wine in an oak barrel. All that is known for certain is that many youthful wines gain not only a more lively flavour and richer colour, but also the ability to retain these qualities for a longer period than an equivalent wine that has not been in wood.

Oak barrels for wine-making are manufactured in Europe and in the United States of America, areas which are home to different species of oak tree. The European oak has porous wood which must be split into wooden staves along the grain for a water- or wine-tight barrel to be made. The tubular effect of the wood's molecular structure must not allow wine to pass sideways through the stave. This restriction means that only 20 per cent of a perfect tree can be used for coopering, and naturally this influences the cost of the barrels.

The wood of American oak trees is less porous, and can be sawn into planks, even across the grain, and then cut into staves that are used for barrel-making. It imparts a more pronounced flavour to the wine than does the European oak, giving wine-makers an additional element to take into consideration when deciding on their preferred wine style.

Oak trees also grow in South Africa, having been brought into the country at the time of the early European settlement. They add decorative effect to the countryside, but their fast-growing timber is too porous for use in barrel-making. Consequently all timber for cask construction in South Africa is imported, either in the form of staves ready for assembly, or as completed barrels.

1. The oak staves chosen to make a barrel are held in place with iron hoops. 2. After the wood has been softened by heat from the fire, the lower hoops are fitted to create the familiar barrel shape. 3. The tubular section of the barrel, now in its final form, is given an additional toasting.

6

7

After felling, the giant oak tree chosen for barrel-making lies on the ground it has over-shadowed for more than two centuries. The massive trunk is sawn into barrel-length cylinders and these in turn are split lengthwise into rough planks about a hand-span wide. Each will be trimmed to make a barrel stave. The planks are stacked high on pallets in the open air and left for several years to season in the sun and rain. The sap leaches out of the timber and the moisture content of the wood drops to that of the air.

To make a barrel, these rectangular staves are tapered at each end. About 30 of them are stood on one end and grouped in the form of a barrel, then held in place by iron hoops. To bend the oak into a curve the staves are exposed to a small wood fire. When hot, the lower ends of the grouped staves are winched or jacked together to create the barrel unit and other iron hoops are hammered into place to hold the staves in this new shape.

The initial heating of the stave creates a lightly singed appearance and gives a mildly toasted flavour to wine stored later in the barrel. Most coopers give the tubular shape a further degree of toasting over a fire at this stage of assembly. Then the circular ends of the barrel are inserted, the working iron hoops are replaced with new galvanised hoops to hold the staves tightly in place, and the barrel's exterior is sanded clean. Finally, water is pumped into the new barrel and the pressure inside is raised to several times that of the atmosphere. When the barrel shows no sign of leaking, it is packed for shipment to a winery.

4. The iron hoops have been replaced by galvanised ones, and the ends are grooved so that the circular head can be fitted. 5. Most French barrels are imported fully assembled. 6. Heating the staves over an oak-chip fire allows them to be bent into shape without breaking. 7. The finished product in use.

The Cape winelands have much to offer the traveller: secluded valleys surrounded by towering mountain crags, historic towns and gracious homesteads set among the vineyards and, not least, the opportunity to sample hundreds of different wines on the farms where they were grown. Most of the region's wine farms are now open for tastings and many provide lunches, enabling guests to try local cuisine in combination with the local wines. Cape wines are becoming known and appreciated throughout the world, but there can be no doubt that the best place to enjoy them is under the sun and among the mountains and people that nurtured them.

GETTING TO KNOW
Cape Wines

The Cape wine routes

To help the traveller explore all the wine-tasting opportunities the Cape winelands have to offer, the region has been divided into localised wine routes, each of which has its own tourist guide and map.

Closest to Cape Town, the wineries in the Constantia valley combine a rich historical heritage with a range of richly flavoured products. Situated on a narrow neck of land between the Atlantic and Indian oceans, they offer visitors an unforgettable introduction to Cape wines and Cape history. Northeastward, en route to Paarl, a small number of wine farms around Durbanville invite travellers to sample their produce in informal surroundings.

To the east, and representing the next oldest settlement after Cape Town, the Stellenbosch wine route boasts 27 estates, private wineries and co-operative cellars which provide wine-tasting facilities as well as restaurants and other attractions. Many of the farms are spectacularly situated, their white Cape Dutch homesteads set against the slopes of the mountains surrounding Stellenbosch. As one of the first farming settlements in the original Dutch colony, the town itself has a large number of historical buildings, including the oldest village

(Previous page) A picnic on the lawns at Boschendal is a highlight of a Cape winelands visit. 1. A school class has a history lesson in Groot Constantia's manor house. 2. A former school building in the suburb of Constantia has become a tasting room where wines of the farm Uitsig may be sampled.

3. The tasting and sales room at Groot Constantia, designed for heavy summer-holiday traffic, seen in the off season. 4. A major feature
of Cape Town's own wine route in suburban Constantia is the house and cellar buildings of Groot Constantia.

home, which dates from 30 years after the town was founded in 1679 and is now a museum, and virtually an entire street of nineteenth-century Cape houses. It is also the seat of a prominent university. In the Stellenbosch area, both in the town and out among the vineyards, there are several dozen restaurants. Some specialise in local food and themes while others show more eclectic influences. During summer a number of wine estates provide alfresco platter lunches which can be enjoyed outside the cellar tasting room. At Spier − one of the district's oldest wine farms which has recently been developed into a major tourist complex with restaurants, wine shop and tasting facilities, conference centre and open-air amphitheatre − you can picnic on the lawns alongside the Eerste River.

Paarl, further north, is the home of the KWV, one of the largest wine and brandy cellars in the world, and of the Nederburg cellars, at which the annual Nederburg Auction is held. Twenty estates and co-operatives around the picturesque town and in the surrounding Berg River valley are members of the Paarl wine route, welcoming visitors to taste their produce.

The Paarl valley has several other attractions for visitors, including the Wiesenhof Game Park and a nearby crocodile farm where baby reptiles destined for breeding programmes are raised to adolescence before being shipped to warmer climates. Cheese lovers can sample some interesting, farm-produced flavours at Fairview, Landskroon and Glen Carlou.

Paarl and nearby Wellington share a heritage of gracious country living and many of the great houses of last century have been converted into fine guesthouses, with award-winning

1. Morgenhof is one of several wineries on the Stellenbosch wine route which offers alfresco lunches. 2. Spier's retail shop displays many Cape wines for sale.
3. An incongruously German-style castle can be seen in the Jonkershoek valley, near Stellenbosch, with a more distant Cape Dutch farm as its neighbour.

chefs running some of the kitchens. Wellington, too, has a wine route, and visitors can taste wine in a Cape Dutch home or in a co-operative's modern cellar.

Higher up the Berg River lies Franschhoek, a pretty town in one of the most beautiful, and fertile, of the Cape's valleys. It was in this high, narrow valley that French Huguenot refugees settled at the end of the seventeenth century and, particularly since the founding of the Franschhoek wine route in 1984, an atmosphere reminiscent of France has been rekindled here. The local wine-makers call themselves the *Vignerons de Franschhoek*, and many of their farms have retained the French names they were originally given. Perhaps not surprisingly, in view of its French connections, the town has developed a reputation for fine dining. The first great country table in the Cape, *Le Quartier Français,* has been joined by several spectacularly sited restaurants that have gained renown far beyond South Africa's borders.

Beyond the Du Toit's Kloof Mountains, Worcester is the hub of another wine route, whose far-flung members are mostly co-operatives producing economically priced wines. A drive to Worcester involves a journey through or over some spectacular mountain scenery. You can choose to ascend the historic Bain's Kloof Pass or the Du Toit's Kloof Pass, or you can

5

4. *All kinds of musical events, from jazz to symphony concerts, are performed in Spier's open-air amphitheatre on warm summer evenings.*

5. *This historic building, today one of Spier's many restaurants, has seen many forms of transport.*

2

3

simply drive through the Huguenot Tunnel. Worcester itself is a thriving business town, and has a very interesting collection of early Cape wine-making, distilling and general farming equipment at the Klein Plasie ('small farm') Museum.

Travelling eastward from Worcester, wine-lovers can sample excellent white and dessert wines along the Robertson route and, even further afield, the celebrated sweet wines of the Little Karoo. The stately homes of this area were built when the fashion for feathers was at its height a century ago and Little Karoo farmers made enormous fortunes from their ostrich flocks. You can still see these great birds grazing in fields adjacent to the vineyards.

South-east of Cape Town, on the coast, are the more recently planted vineyard areas near Hermanus and Bot River, where visitors can combine the pleasures of wine-tasting with whale-watching and the holiday pastimes of a coastal resort. The wine farms here are the most southerly in South Africa, and the vines, benefiting from cooling sea breezes in summer and plentiful rainfall, produce wines of excellent quality.

Of two west coast wine routes north of Cape Town, the Swartland route is closer to the city, its members, mainly co-operatives, lying scattered around the town of Malmesbury. Beyond it the Olifants River wine route stretches to the river's lower reaches, where the irrigated vineyards contrast vividly with their arid surroundings. Vredendal is the focal point of this most northerly wine route, where all except one of the half-dozen members are co-operatives. Each cellar produces vast quantities of grapes which make up a substantial proportion of the Cape's annual crop.

The semi-desert climate of the west coast allows open-air dining virtually all year round, and the seafood-rich Benguela current provides delicacies for traditional Cape dishes of the area's outdoor restaurants, some of which are situated right on the beach.

1   4

1. The kilometre-long avenue of stone pines leading to the Neethlingshof house and cellar is a landmark of the Stellenbosch wine route. 2. Muratie's charming old buildings show how the Cape's great farms looked half a century ago. 3. The tasting room and visitors' reception at Overgaauw, near Stellenbosch. 4. Old-time Stellenbosch shopping is re-created in the commercial activities of Oom Samie se Winkel (Uncle Samie's Shop) in Dorp Street.

Shows, auctions and festivals

Wine shows have not traditionally been a major feature on the Cape calendar. Until comparatively recently, most wine brands were owned by trading companies which bought wines from co-operatives and blended them. The best of these wines were – and still are – displayed each year at a series of regional young wine shows where tank samples of the new vintage are judged. To meet the needs of consumers more interested in the product which has already been blended, matured and bottled, the Stellenbosch Bottled Wine Show and later the South African Bottled Wine Show were inaugurated in the 1980s. Today the Veritas awards bestowed at the national event are probably the leading indicators of excellence in the Cape wine industry.

1

Two commercial organisations, Diners Club and South African Airways, make a major contribution not only to bringing the best of the Cape wines to the consumers' attention, but also to motivating wine-makers. Each year South African Airways appoints five local and five international judges to determine which of the Cape wines will be included on the air service's onboard winelist. The Diners Club Wine-maker of the Year Award is more specific, focusing on a different type of wine each year. The forthcoming year's category is announced in advance, allowing wine-makers to experiment with and polish their product.

Auctions and sales of rare and sought-after wines are less common in South Africa than they are elsewhere in the world, but the Cape does boast the internationally-known Nederburg Auction which has been held annually since 1975. The organisers select a number of batches of scarce bottlings of wine from the top Cape producers and sell these under the hammer along with many small-volume lots of Nederburg's own rare bottlings. Held at

2

3

1. Nederburg's annual wine auction brings trade buyers from many world markets. 2. At the estate Rhebokskloof, just north of Paarl, diners on the attractive stoep can look down onto the farm dam. 3. Roggeland Country House, outside Paarl, is one of the Cape's premier country guesthouses.

4

5

the end of March or beginning of April each year, the auction has become a highlight on the Cape's social calendar.

The Cape Independent Winemakers' Guild organises a different type of showcase – a barrel tasting – later in the year, usually in August. The guild members generally make and sell their own wines, and as a group have been in the forefront of vineyard and cellar technology advances over the past few years. They supply prize-quality wine to the barrel tasting for interested consumers to sample and compare. At the same time, there is an auction of selected products made by members exclusively for the event.

Throughout the Cape, people of the winelands are as keen to celebrate their wines as to make them. The year of festivals for wine-lovers and wine-producers alike begins with St. Vincent's Eve, held late in January to celebrate the harvesting of grapes for *cap classique* sparkling wines. When the main activity of picking, crushing and fermenting is over, it is time to celebrate the harvest. Towards the end of March the farm Eikendal opens its gates to visitors to observe the *Weintaufe*, or 'baptising' of the wine. April heralds the Paarl Nouveau Festival, and the winter months of May and June bring a series of village food and wine fêtes throughout the countryside. July features the national port festival in the Little Karoo, and then the last few months of the year witness the Stellenbosch Food and Wine Festival, followed by celebrations in the small, wine-producing valleys of Tulbagh and McGregor.

4. Paarl celebrates the launch of the nouveau reds from the valley's cellars with a theme festival each April. 5. The farm Fairview was one of the pioneers of goats' milk cheese production. This novel housing for the goats is in front of the winery.

Cape cuisine

With a heritage of combined cooking styles from East and West that has developed over three centuries, South Africa's indigenous cuisine has longer and more widely established traditions than most New World cultures. The varied cuisines that may be found in most western urban areas are also prevalent in the Cape, but have been incorporated into a rich and complex local food lore.

The first visitors to the Cape who decided to stay, the Dutch, brought two major kitchen influences to Table Bay: their own and one from the East. Through conquest in the seventeenth century, they had become rulers of the greater part of what is today Indonesia and Eastern India, and by shipping spices back to their home country they developed a taste for oriental flavours still evident today. Ships travelling east and west between Holland and its eastern holdings brought influences and ingredients from both destinations to the Cape.

Moreover, the Dutch settled people from their Eastern colonies at the Cape, and these often highly educated and skilled people were incorporated into the Cape labour force as artisans, fishermen, seamstresses and cooks. The women brought with them knowledge of the traditional uses of the precious Eastern spices that were carried by the passing Dutch East Indian ships and soon became the building blocks of what is known today as Cape Malay cooking. After the arrival of the British administration in 1806 and the consequent conclusion of Dutch-Indonesian trade at the Cape, some of the ingredients became too scarce for everyday use and spices like saffron and green ginger were replaced by locally available flavouring agents such as orange leaves and dried apricots.

The Eastern slaves and their descendants were the first important fishermen at the Cape. They learnt to dry, smoke and salt fish, and the Cape Malay food culture has a strong accent on seafood. Other influences came to Cape cooking with various European settlers, notably the French Huguenots, but Cape Malay has remained the only original development. Today the wealth of agricultural produce from the land and the harvests from the adjacent oceans ensure that the creativity of future generations of cooks have plenty of opportunity to build on this rich culinary tradition.

1

2

3

4

5

1. Traditional Cape cooking lends itself to buffet-style presentation, as seen at Boschendal, on the Franschhoek wine route. 2. The Cape's warm, dry summers encourage leisurely outdoor dining. 3. Franschhoek boasts many small wineries, some of which have christened their wines with inventive style. 4. At the Franschhoek Co-operative Winery many of the wines of the valley can be tried. 5. Haute Cabrière's cellar features a fine restaurant with a glorious view. It can be hired for special functions.

Appreciating wines

Every new and developing wine culture attracts enthusiastic students, and the Cape culture, currently in the most dynamic period of its existence, is no exception. It boasts a privately funded school of wine knowledge that is the envy of other cultures. Founded in 1979, the Cape Wine Academy was originally designed to provide a forum for teachers and students, and to enhance knowledge of the world of wine among producers and the trade. It soon became clear that it found greatest support among wine consumers in general, who are eager to learn all they can about the wine industry and how best to appreciate its products.

Courses provided by the Cape Wine Academy teach a basic understanding of wine production and marketing to assist newcomers to the trade. At progressively more difficult standards they impart knowledge about wines and their presentation, with regular examinations enabling enthusiasts to reach and overcome the final hurdle of the Cape Wine Master test.

In common with most New World wine-producing countries, South Africa has hundreds of private wine appreciation clubs at which members add to their knowledge of wines using the principle of self-help. Every year they can try out what they have learned at the Blaauwklippen Blending Competition, where they are given a theme and blending components to make wines of their own.

1. Intensive vine cultivation in the Robertson valley is carried out by more than a dozen wineries, many of which have tasting rooms.

2. The tea-room in the Mamre mission village, near Darling on the west coast, is reminiscent of country life in the last century.

3

4

3. Dining at one of several beach restaurants along the west coast, where more than 20 different types of seafood are on offer, is an experience that shouldn't
be missed. 4. Ostrich farming and wine farming go together in the Little Karoo, where the big birds can be seen grazing alongside the vineyards.

119

INDEX

Page numbers in *italic* refer to photographs.